FOCUS ON

MIDDLE SCHOOL

ASTRONOMY

Rebecca W. Keller, PhD

REAL SCIENCE 4 Kids

Illustrations: Rebecca W. Keller, PhD, Janet Moneymaker, Marjie Bassler
Editor: Marjie Bassler

Focus On Middle School Astronomy Student Textbook (softcover)

ISBN #978-1-936114-47-4

Published by Gravitas Publications, Inc.
www.gravitaspublications.com

Printed in United States

GRAVITAS
PUBLICATIONS

Contents

Chapter 1 What Is Astronomy?

1.1 Introduction

Astronomy is considered by many to be the oldest science. Since long before the invention of the telescope, human beings have been looking at the stars. The word astronomy (ə-strä'-nə-mē) comes from the Greek word *aster* which means "star" and the Greek word *nomas* which means "to assign, distribute, or arrange." The word astronomy literally means "to assign or arrange the stars." Astronomers are scientists who assign names to all the celestial (sə-les'-chəl) bodies in space, including stars, and study how they exist and move in space.

1.2 Early Astronomers

The earliest recorded history reveals an interest in the stars. Cave drawings show primitive humans recording observations from the skies, and later the Babylonians (ba-bə-lō'-nyənz) recorded detailed planetary positions, eclipses, and other astronomical observations. Egyptian and Greek observers expanded on the information collected by the Babylonians. The alignment of the pyramids with the North Star suggests that the Egyptians acquired sophisticated abilities to observe the sky. The Ancient Greeks were the first astronomers to add mathematics to astronomy.

Many early civilizations used the stars and the movements of celestial bodies as tools to measure time. The Sumerians (sü-mer'-ē-ənz) of Babylonia used the phases of the Moon to create the first lunar calendar, and the Egyptians, Greeks, and Romans copied and revised this calendar. Today our calendar is derived directly from the Sumerian calendar and is connected to the monthly and yearly orbits of the Moon and Earth. On the other side of the ocean, the Incan and Mayan civilizations created sophisticated calendars by observing the planetary cycles. The Mayan calendar is circular and has aspects that relate the movement of the Sun, Moon and planets.

Early astronomers named individual stars as well as groups of stars that form constellations (kän-stə-lā'-shənz). A constellation is any group of stars that fit together to form a pattern in the night sky. Some of the major constellations that come from Greek mythology are familiar to many people. Orion (ə-rī'-ən) the Hunter is a constellation of stars that can be seen from the northern hemisphere from December through March. Orion has a "belt" of three bright stars in a straight row. Once the "belt" is located, it is easy to find the "club" and "shield" by looking for neighboring stars.

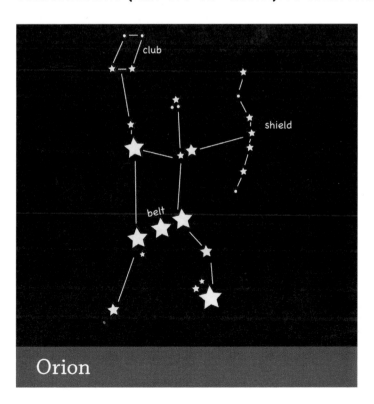

Orion

The constellation names derived from Greek mythology have changed very little since 1000 BC (BCE). There are currently 88 constellations that are recognized by the International Astronomical Union (IAU), and over half of those were observed by the ancient Greeks!

1.3 Modern Astronomers

Today, astronomers can see many more stars than their ancient predecessors could. Modern astronomers can also see details about the planets and stars that were not visible in ancient times.

In Chapter 2 we will look closely at the tools a modern astronomer uses to look at celestial bodies. Telescopes, radios, and cameras are just some of the tools astronomers use when studying the planets and stars. Modern astronomers also use chemistry and physics to understand astronomical data. Understanding how planets move requires knowing the physics behind gravity, inertia, and mass. Understanding how stars give off heat and light energy requires knowing the chemistry behind nuclear reactions. And understanding how the Sun affects our weather requires knowledge of magnetic and electric fields. Modern astronomers not only have sophisticated tools to explore the universe, they also have centuries of complicated mathematics, chemistry, and physics to help them understand how the universe works.

1.4 Changing Views of the Cosmos

The practice of astronomy changed dramatically after the invention of the telescope, a scientific tool that uses lenses to magnify distant objects. In the 1600's Galileo (ga-lə-lā'-ō), an Italian scientist considered to be the first modern astronomer, used the telescope to look at the planets. Galileo was also able to see the moons of Jupiter and the rotation of the Sun. Based on his observations, Galileo confirmed a radical new view of the cosmos (käz'-mōs). The cosmos, or solar system, includes our Sun and the planets around it.

In ancient times most people believed that the Earth was the center of the universe. These ancients believed that the planets and the Sun moved in a circular orbit, or path, around the Earth. This view of the world is called geocentric (jē-ō-sen'-trik). Geo comes from the Greek word *ge* which means "earth" or "land"and centric comes from the Greek word *kentron* which means "point" or "center." A geocentric view is one that considers the Earth as the true center of the universe.

Geocentric Cosmos

It is not hard to understand why this view was held. Stepping outside at any given time of the day and observing the motion of the Sun, it *looks like* the Sun rotates around the Earth. A geocentric view of the universe was first proposed by Aristotle (a'-rə-stä-təl) (384-322 BC [BCE]) and was the dominant belief held by most people for many centuries.

However, not everyone agreed with Aristotle. Aristarchus of Samos (a-rə-stär'-kəs of sā'-mäs), who lived from 310-230 BC (BCE), was an expert Greek astronomer and mathematician who did not believe that the Sun and planets revolved around the Earth. He was the first to propose a heliocentric (hē-lē-ō-sen'-trik) cosmos. The word heliocentric comes from the Greek word *helios* which means "sun." A heliocentric cosmos is a view of the universe with the Sun as the central point and the Earth and planets orbiting the Sun.

Heliocentric Cosmos

Although today we know that Aristarchus was right, his proposal was rejected by his colleagues because it seemed to contradict everyday observation. If the Earth was not stable (central and not moving), how did everything not bolted down keep from flying off the Earth as it rotated around the Sun? The physics of Aristotle was the scientific consensus view during Aristarchus' lifetime and that meant that a heliocentric cosmos would have violated the laws of physics! It was almost 2000 years before the idea of a heliocentric cosmos was reintroduced by Nicolaus Copernicus (kō-pər'-ni-kəs) (1473-1543) and confirmed by the scientific observations of Galileo.

Today, astronomers do not believe in a geocentric cosmos and know that our Earth orbits the Sun and that we live in a heliocentric solar system. Modern technologies, a deeper understanding of physics, and a willingness to challenge prevailing scientific theories were needed before the geocentric view could be replaced by the more accurate heliocentric view of the cosmos.

1.5 Summary

- Astronomy is the field of science that studies celestial bodies and how they exist and move in space.

- Early astronomers were able to map the movements of the planets and stars and used celestial motions to create calendars.

- Modern astronomers use chemistry and physics together with modern technologies to study the universe.

- Ancient peoples once believed in a geocentric cosmos, or Earth-centered universe. Today we know that we live in a heliocentric solar system with the Sun at the center.

Chapter 2 Astronomers' Toolbox

2.1 Introduction

Now that we have seen how the science of astronomy began, we can take a look at the tools astronomers use to explore the skies. Tools are an essential part of scientific investigation, and for hundreds of centuries astronomers have been using tools to gain a better understanding of the universe.

Even before the invention of the telescope, early astronomers used tools to study the sky. In the 1500s BC (BCE) ancient civilizations used tools to track the movement of the Sun. Stonehenge, a group of huge stones set in a circular shape outside of Amesbury, England, is believed to be a kind of solar tracking system. As the Sun moves over the large structure, the shadows mark the summer and winter solstices.

Stonehenge, near Amesbury, England

Today, modern astronomy tools help scientists get accurate readings of star or planetary movements and help them observe stellar objects that they can't see with their eyes. In this chapter we will learn about some of the tools modern astronomers use.

2.2 Telescopes

When Galileo decided to look at the night sky, he used a telescope. The word telescope comes from the Greek prefix *tele-* which means "from afar" or "far off" and *skopein* which means to "see," "watch," or "view." A telescope is an instrument used to see, watch, or view things that are far away.

Galileo is sometimes credited with the invention of the telescope, but in 1608 the Dutch lens maker, Hans Lippershey, filed the first patent for what would eventually become the telescope. Galileo made many improvements to the Dutch "perspective lens" and was able to greatly increase the magnification. With his powerful lenses, Galileo was able to see all the moons of Jupiter!

There are essentially three types of telescopes: refractor telescopes, reflector telescopes, and compound telescopes.

The first telescopes built were refractor telescopes. Refractor telescopes can be found in hobby and toy stores and are the type of telescopes used for rifles.

A refractor telescope houses a lens at one end and an eyepiece at the opposite end of a narrow tube. Light enters one end of the tube and is bent by the lens. The observer looks through the tube from the opposite end and sees the magnified object at the focal point, the spot at which the rays of light entering the lens come together to produce the image.

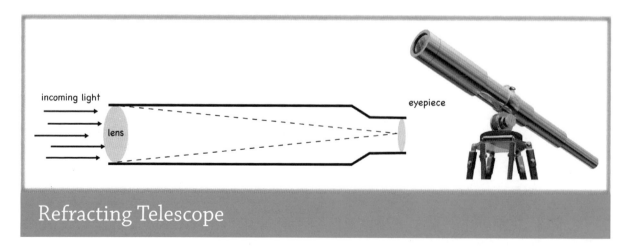

incoming light

lens

eyepiece

Refracting Telescope

The largest refracting telescope ever constructed was at the Great Paris Exhibition in 1900. It had a focal length (the distance from a lens to its focal point) of 57 meters (187 feet) but was later dismantled after the company went bankrupt. Today the largest refracting telescope in use is housed at the Yerkes Observatory in Chicago.

Yerkes Observatory, Chicago, IL, USA

Reflector telescopes and compound telescopes use a combination of mirrors and lenses to focus incoming light. These telescopes are more complicated than the refractor telescope and can provide better quality images. A common reflector telescope is the Newtonian telescope named after its inventor, Isaac Newton. A Newtonian telescope has a simple design with two mirrors and an eyepiece. Light enters the telescope at the far end, is reflected back by one mirror, and hits a second mirror where it exits to the eyepiece.

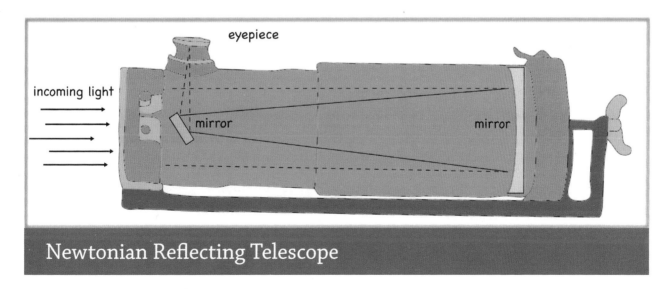

Newtonian Reflecting Telescope

2.3 Space Tools

Although telescopes can be built to see planets and stars that are millions of miles away, Earth's atmosphere causes problems for making observations from the Earth's surface. Light coming from a distant star must pass through the Earth's atmosphere (the air) before it can be collected by a telescope on the surface. As the light passes through the atmosphere, it can be reflected by tiny atmospheric particles. Atmospheric turbulence causes these particles to move, creating small changes in the optical properties of the air. Before it

enters a telescope, the light that is being collected gets bounced around, which makes it appear that the image of the object being viewed is moving. This also makes stars appear to "twinkle." Although twinkling stars are fun to watch, they prevent astronomers from collecting the kind of detailed data that is needed for study.

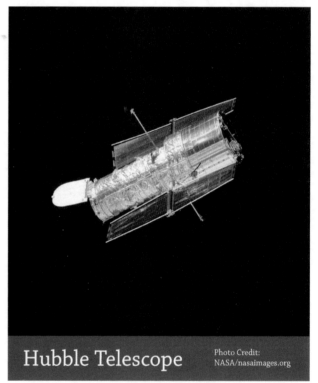

Hubble Telescope   Photo Credit: NASA/nasaimages.org

A great way to solve this problem is to set up a telescope outside the Earth's atmosphere. The Hubble Space Telescope is one such telescope. It was placed into orbit by the Discovery shuttle in 1990. The Hubble Telescope is able to take sharp and detailed images of many distant objects with very little distortion. Our understanding of the universe has been expanded as a result of images taken by the Hubble Telescope.

Space probes, landers, and rovers are other tools used by scientists to explore space.

A space probe is a robotic spaceship that can travel far distances, capturing images and collecting data. *Voyager 1* is a space probe that was launched in

Viking 1

Photo Credit:
NASA/nasaimages.org

1977 and is still being used to explore space well beyond our solar system.

A lander is a robotic spaceship, like a space probe, but it is able to land on the surface of planets or asteroids (small celestial bodies made mostly of rock and minerals). The first image of the surface of Mars was captured by the lander *Viking 1*, which landed on Mars in July 1976 and continued collecting data for six years.

A rover is lander that can move. A rover is an automated machine that can travel across a planetary surface. Since the mid 1990s several rovers have landed on Mars. The first was *Sojourner* in 1997 followed by *Spirit* and *Opportunity* in 2004. Although *Opportunity* continues to collect data, *Spirit* became stuck in the sand, and in March 2010, it stopped transmitting data. The most recent Mars rover is *Curiosity* which was launched in November 2011.

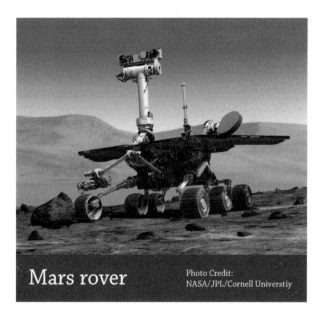

Mars rover

Photo Credit:
NASA/JPL/Cornell Universtiy

2.4 Summary

- Astronomers use tools to explore the cosmos.

- Telescopes are used to magnify far away objects.

- Modern astronomers can utilize space tools to collect data. Space probes, landers, and rovers are among the tools used.

Chapter 3 Earth in Space

3.1 Introduction

Now that we know what astronomy is and what tools astronomers use to examine the stars in the sky, we can start looking at celestial objects in space. The first object in space that we will explore is Earth itself.

What is the shape of the Earth? Is it flat, round, elliptical? Where does the Earth sit with respect to the larger universe? Is it in the middle, off to the side, on the outer edge? In this chapter we will explore these questions and others as we examine the Earth in space.

3.2 The Earth in Space

The ancient Greeks understood that the Earth is a ball, or spherical mass. The best evidence in ancient times for the Earth being spherical came from the observation that a circular shadow is cast during a lunar eclipse. The ancient Greeks could see the curvature of Earth from its shadow on the Moon.

However, it was only within the last 100 years that we have been able to photograph the Earth in space. The very first pictures of Earth as seen from space were taken in 1946 by a group of scientists in New Mexico. These scientists attached a 35 millimeter camera to a missile and launched the missile 65 miles into space. The missile came crashing down, but the film was protected in a tough metal container. The crude black and white photos showed the curvature of the Earth and marked a new era for space exploration.

Earth is a planet. The word planet comes from the Greek word *planetai* which means "wanderer." A planet is a large spherical object or celestial body that "wanders" in space. To qualify as a planet, a celestial body must orbit a sun, must have enough mass to have its own gravity, and must have cleared its orbit of other celestial bodies. Because Earth "wanders," or moves in space, around the Sun, is massive enough to have its own gravity, and also has cleared its orbit, Earth qualifies as a planet.

At the equator, Earth is 12,756 kilometers (7,926 miles) in diameter. Between the North Pole and the South Pole it is 12,714 kilometers (7,900 miles) in diameter. You can see that Earth is not a perfect sphere but is slightly larger in one dimension.

Earth sits on a tilted axis, which is the imaginary line around which the Earth rotates. Having a tilted axis means that the North and South Poles are not straight up and down in relation to the Earth's orbit around the Sun. If you were to look at the planetary axis, you would see that the poles are tilted about 23 degrees from center. This deviation from perpendicular is called orbital obliquity (ō-bli'-kwə-tē). Orbital obliquity, the tilt of Earth's axis, gives us the seasons.

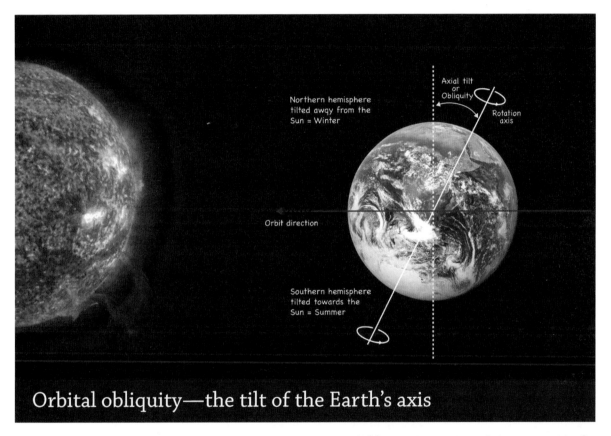

Orbital obliquity—the tilt of the Earth's axis

As the Earth spins, or rotates, on its axis, different parts of the Earth face toward or away from the Sun. The Earth actually makes one full rotation around its axis in slightly less than 24 hours, at 23.93 hours. This rotation on a roughly 24 hour cycle gives us our days and nights.

During different seasons of the year, the North and South Poles get more sunlight or less sunlight than the areas around the equator because the tilt of the axis points a pole toward or away from the Sun. Because of this, the poles can have nearly 24 hours of sunlight or 24 hours of darkness. So, not all days and nights are equal everywhere on the planet.

3.3 The Earth and the Moon

The Earth has one moon. A moon is any celestial body that orbits a planet. A moon is also called a natural satellite. The word moon comes from the Greek word *menas* which means month. The Moon orbits the Earth and completes one orbit every 27 days (roughly one month), hence its name—the "Moon."

The Moon can be seen from Earth because the Moon reflects light from the Sun. As the Moon orbits the Earth and as both the Earth and the Moon orbit the Sun, the appearance of the Moon changes. We call these changes phases.

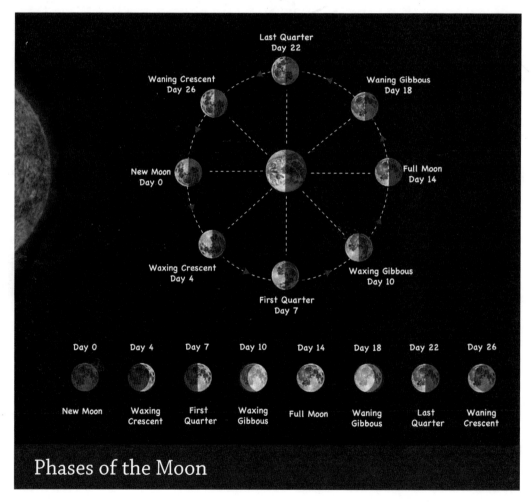

Phases of the Moon

In the first phase, on Day 0, the Moon is called a new moon. The new moon occurs when the Moon is between the Earth and the Sun. Only the back side of the Moon is illuminated by the Sun, so from Earth the Moon looks dark.

As the Moon continues to orbit the Earth, by Day 4 it enters the next phase called the waxing crescent moon. From Earth, only a small portion of the Moon appears illuminated and is crescent shaped. By Day 7 the Moon moves to the next phase and appears half-illuminated, This is called the first quarter moon, or "half-moon." A few days later, on Day 10, the Moon moves to the waxing gibbous (ji'-bəs) phase. A gibbous moon is between a full moon and a quarter moon. The word gibbous means "marked by convexity or swelling," so a gibbous moon is a moon that looks "swollen."

By Day 14, the Moon enters the full moon phase. The Moon is now on the opposite side of the Earth from the Sun and is seen with full illumination. A few days later, by Day 18, the Moon becomes a waning gibbous moon. Then, by Day 22, it enters the next to last phase, the last quarter moon, when the Moon is again half-illuminated, but now the illumination appears on the opposite side from the first quarter moon. Finally, by Day 26 the Moon enters the last phase, becoming a waning crescent moon. By Day 30 the Moon is back to being a new moon and the cycle repeats.

Phases of the Moon
Image credit: NASA/nasaimages.org

The Moon and the Earth interact with each other through long range gravitational forces. Recall from *Focus On Middle School Physics* that any object that has mass (the property that makes matter resist being moved) also has gravitational force (the force exerted by objects on one another). Your body has mass and also a small amount of gravitational force. But because you are very small compared to the Earth, your gravitational force does not affect the Earth.

The Moon is much bigger than you. But it has much less mass than the Earth and therefore has less gravitational force. However, the Moon has enough mass to create a gravitational pull on the Earth.

The Moon has dramatic effects on Earth. For example, the Moon is believed to stabilize Earth's rotation and the tilt of its axis. Without a moon, the Earth might swing more dramatically between degrees of obliquity, unable to maintain an average tilt of 23 degrees. If the Earth tilted more or less dramatically, this could result in extreme or even catastrophic seasons.

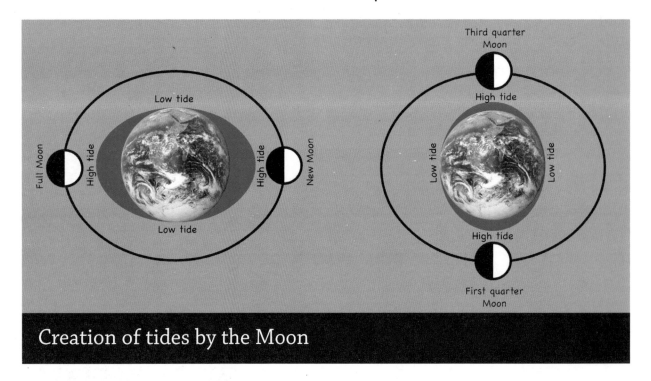

Creation of tides by the Moon

The Moon also contributes to the rise and fall of ocean tides. Ocean tides on Earth are created in part by the gravitational forces exerted by the Moon. The Moon (together with the Sun) pulls on the Earth's center, which creates two tidal bulges. As the Earth rotates on its own axis, these bulges are dragged along the Earth's surface, causing the sea level to rise and fall, thus creating tides.

3.4 The Earth and the Sun

The Sun is a celestial body in space. It provides the Earth with power. The Sun is like a big battery that never runs out, continuously giving us energy in the form of light and heat. From this energy, life is possible. Without the Sun there would be no plants, animals, reptiles, fish, or even microbes. All of life requires energy in order to move, grow, eat, and reproduce. Every chemical reaction in your body requires energy, and it is ultimately the Sun's energy that powers the chemical reactions in your body.

Not only does the Sun power our planet, it also interacts with Earth, affecting tides, weather, and even our magnetic field. We saw in the last section how the Moon pulls on the Earth causing tides in our oceans. The Sun also pulls on the Earth causing tidal activity.

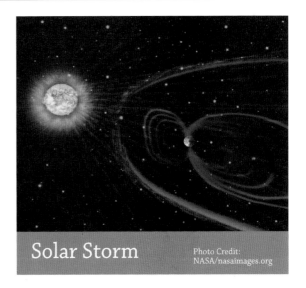

Solar Storm

Photo Credit: NASA/nasaimages.org

Did you know that "space weather" affects our own weather on Earth? It's easy to forget that Earth is not a closed system. We are a blue ball in space, interacting with other space objects like planets and the Sun. The Sun affects our planet in major ways, and one way is the weather.

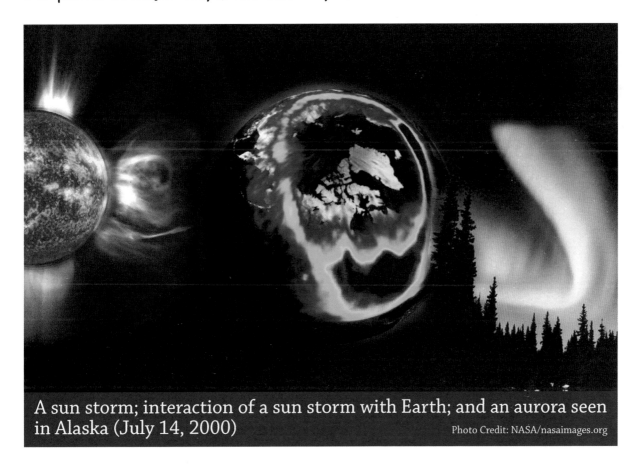

A sun storm; interaction of a sun storm with Earth; and an aurora seen in Alaska (July 14, 2000)

Photo Credit: NASA/nasaimages.org

Weather can be tough to predict on Earth. You might not think that a solar storm on the Sun could cause a storm on our planet, yet this is exactly what happens. Earth's weather is caused by temperature and moisture variations in different places. When the Sun has a solar storm and a burst of heat escapes, we get a rise in temperature on Earth, which can then create storms.

The Sun also interacts with Earth's atmosphere causing auroras (ə-rôr′-əz), which are sometimes called northern lights and southern lights. Auroras are caused by solar storms that charge particles in space. These charged particles get trapped by Earth's magnetic field. When this happens, they pass through our atmosphere and give off light as they release energy.

3.5 Eclipses

There are two types of eclipses that can occur. A lunar eclipse occurs when the Moon passes directly behind the Earth and the Earth blocks the Sun's rays from illuminating the Moon. The Moon is darkened as the Sun's rays are blocked and the Earth's shadow passes across the Moon.

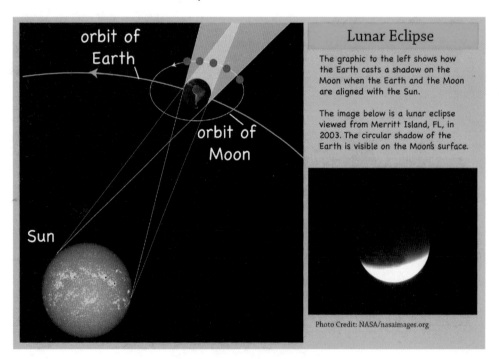

orbit of Earth

orbit of Moon

Sun

Lunar Eclipse

The graphic to the left shows how the Earth casts a shadow on the Moon when the Earth and the Moon are aligned with the Sun.

The image below is a lunar eclipse viewed from Merritt Island, FL, in 2003. The circular shadow of the Earth is visible on the Moon's surface.

Photo Credit: NASA/nasaimages.org

The other type of eclipse is called a solar eclipse. A solar eclipse occurs when the Moon passes between the Sun and the Earth, blocking the Sun's rays from reaching some location on Earth.

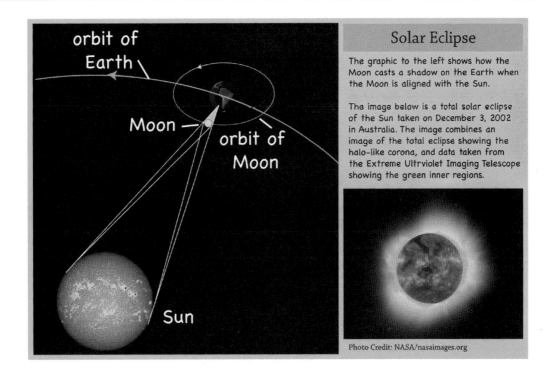

It is tempting to look at a solar eclipse with your naked eye. However, it is very dangerous to look at the eclipse directly. Special glasses or projection techniques must always be used to view a solar eclipse.

3.6 Summary

● The Earth is a celestial body, or planet. The word planet means "wanderer." Earth is called a planet because it rotates around the Sun, has enough mass to have its own gravity, and has cleared its orbit.

● Earth rotates on a tilted axis. This tilt is called orbital obliquity. The rotation of Earth on its axis gives us night and day, and orbital obliquity creates the different seasons.

● The Earth has one moon orbiting it. The Moon stabilizes the tilt and rotation of Earth and contributes to the activity of the tides.

● The Earth orbits the Sun. The Sun provides Earth with energy and contributes to Earth's weather and tidal activity.

Chapter 4 The Moon and the Sun

4.1 Introduction

As we saw in Chapter 3, the Moon and the Sun play an important role in many of Earth's properties, including the Earth's stability, rotation, weather, and tidal actions. In this chapter, as we move away from the Earth and start exploring space, we will take a closer look at the Moon and the Sun.

4.2 The Moon

As we saw in Chapter 3, the word "moon" comes from the Greek word *menas* which means month. We call our moon the "Moon" because it orbits the Earth in a monthly cycle, but not all moons orbit their planets in a monthly cycle. (We will learn more about planets in Chapter 5.)

The adjective lunar is also used to refer to the Moon. Lunar comes from the Latin word *luceo* which means "to shine bright." Although the Moon does not create its own light, it reflects the Sun's light and is the brightest object in the evening sky.

The Moon

The Moon is not made of green cheese. In fact, the Moon is made of elements and minerals, just like Earth. We know that the surface of the Moon is made of elements and minerals because Moon samples were collected by the Apollo astronauts. Moon soil contains aluminum, calcium, iron, magnesium, silicon, and titanium.

There are at least two different types of Moon rocks, basaltic (bə-sôlt´-ik) rocks and breccia (bre´-chē-ə). Basaltic rocks are formed from hardened lava coming from lunar volcanoes, and rocks called breccia come from soil and pieces of rock that have been squeezed by falling objects such as meteors.

The Moon has little or no atmosphere, and in fact, the space around the Moon is close to being a vacuum, which means it is empty of matter. The result of the lack of atmosphere is that there is no weather on the Moon. There are no clouds, rain, or wind. However, water in the form of ice has been discovered below the surface of the Moon.

The Moon is about 3.5 times smaller than the Earth, with a diameter of 3475 kilometers (2158 miles). However, in our solar system it is relatively the largest moon compared to the size of the planet orbited.

The Earth and the Moon
Photo Credit:
NASA/nasaimages.org

Because the Moon has less mass than Earth, it also has less gravity. The gravitational force on the Moon is about one sixth the gravitational force on Earth.

It takes the Moon the same number of days to complete one rotation on its axis as it takes the Moon to make one orbit around the Earth. This means that as the Moon is going around the Earth, the side of the Moon that faces the Earth is slowly rotating at exactly the same rate that the Moon is orbiting the Earth. Therefore, the Moon always has the same side facing the Earth.

The temperature on the Moon varies wildly because it has no atmosphere. During the day, temperatures can be as high as 173 degrees Celsius (280 degrees Fahrenheit). At night, the temperature can dip to as low as -240 degrees C (-400 degrees F).

If you look up at the Moon, you will see both light and dark areas on the surface. The light areas are known as terrae (ter'-ē). The word terrae is Latin and means "lands." These light areas are rugged with craters that can exceed 40 kilometers (25 miles) in diameter.

The dark areas on the Moon are known as maria (mär'-ē-ə). The word maria comes from the Latin word *marinus* which means "sea." When 17th century astronomers were looking at the Moon through their telescopes, they thought that the large dark areas were bodies of water, or seas.

The early astronomers gave the maria fun names such as *Mare Tranquillitatis*, meaning "The Sea of Tranquility," and *Mare Nectaris*, meaning "The Sea of Nectar." Modern astronomers still use these names but know that the dark areas of the Moon are not seas. Instead, these dark areas are lava flows.

The Moon has a crust (an outer, rocky shell), a mantle (the layer below the crust), and an iron-rich core like the Earth. However, the Moon has no magnetic field or "moving plates" like Earth. Scientists believe that the small iron core of the Moon is not large enough to create a magnetic field on the Moon. Also, because of this small core and no moving plates, there is very little seismic (sīz'-mik) activity on the Moon (in other words, there are very few earthquakes).

The Moon—crust and interior

4.3 The Sun

As we saw in Chapter 3, the Sun affects Earth's tides, weather, stability and rotation. But what is the Sun?

The Sun is different from both the Earth and Moon. The sun is a star.

A star is a celestial body that generates light and heat energy. Our star, the Sun, is composed mainly of hydrogen and helium. Hydrogen and helium are the lightest elements known and are gases. Hence, one way to think about the Sun is to imagine it as a hot ball of gas.

Although the Sun is made of lightweight gases, the Sun's diameter is about 100 times the diameter of the Earth, and the Sun is over three hundred thousand times as massive as the Earth.

Mass of Sun/Mass of Earth
= 332,840

To get an idea of just how large the Sun is compared to the Earth, know that about 1 million Earths will fit inside the Sun!

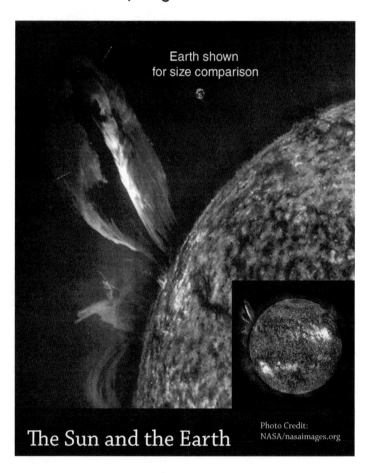

The Sun and the Earth

Photo Credit:
NASA/nasaimages.org

The Sun's temperature is extremely hot, averaging 5800 degrees kelvin (5510 degrees Celsius or 9900 degrees Fahrenheit) with some regions exceeding tens of thousands or even millions of degrees kelvin. Life on Earth is made possible by the extreme temperatures on the Sun that radiate into space. But how does the Sun generate so much energy?

4.4 Chemistry and Physics of Stars

To understand how the Sun can provide the energy to fuel our planet, it is important to look at the chemistry and physics of stars. (More in-depth information on the chemistry and physics presented in this book can be found in the *Focus On Middle School Chemistry Student Textbook* and the *Focus On Middle School Physics Student Textbook*.)

As we saw in Section 4.3, the Sun is composed largely of hydrogen and helium, two lightweight gases. When gases are compressed, their temperature increases. If you hold your hand on a tire tube as you pump air into it, you will find that the tube gets warm. This is heat generated by the increasing pressure imposed on the gas (air).

The Sun is a huge ball of compressed gases and has extremely high temperatures at its center. It is believed that these temperatures are so high that the hydrogen atoms become ionized. Ionization is a process where the electrons and nucleus of an atom become separated. Since a hydrogen atom is made of one proton, one electron, and no neutrons, when hydrogen ionizes, it is converted to a free proton (the nucleus) and a free electron. The proton is positively charged and the electron is negatively charged.

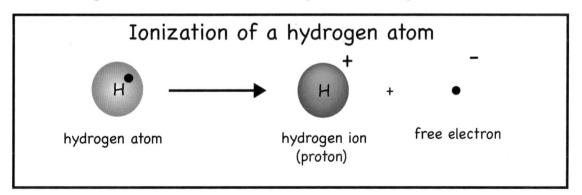

Ionization of a hydrogen atom

hydrogen atom   hydrogen ion (proton)   free electron

What happens when free hydrogen protons meet? We know that when two like charges meet they will repel each other. However, at the extreme pressure and temperature that exist at the center of the Sun, when two hydrogen protons meet, they combine, or fuse, together. This process is called hydrogen fusion. The fusing together of two protons is also called thermonuclear fusion because it can take place only at extremely high temperatures.

However, not only do the two hydrogen protons fuse, but one of the two is converted into a neutron. Eventually, four hydrogen protons (nuclei) will fuse to make a single helium atom.

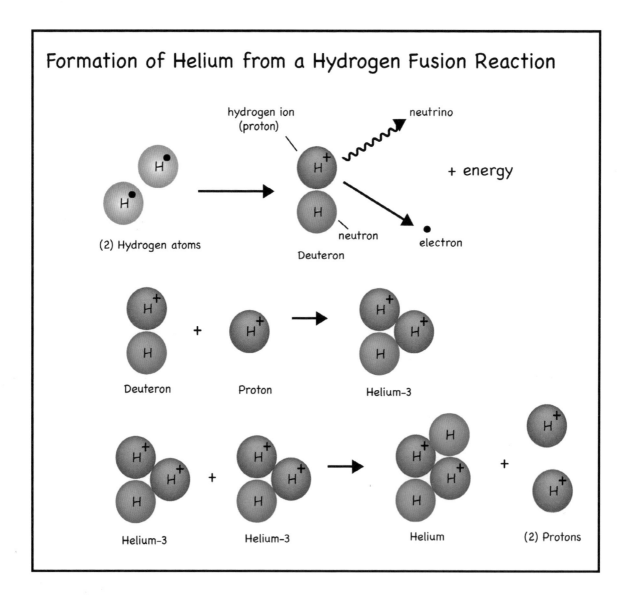

Formation of Helium from a Hydrogen Fusion Reaction

Thermonuclear fusion is a nuclear reaction that releases massive amounts of energy. In 1905 Albert Einstein showed that mass can be converted to energy with his elegantly simple equation:

$$E = mc^2$$

The symbol "E" represents "energy," the symbol "m" represents "mass," and the symbol "c" represents "the speed of light." Because the speed of light is a very large number (c = 299,792,458 x meters/seconds) and is multiplied times itself ("c^2") and then multiplied times the mass ("m"), only a small amount of mass is needed to create large amounts of energy.

For example, if you had a mass ("m") of one gram of hydrogen, using the formula E=mc^2 you would get a result of 21,480,248,771,809 calories of energy ("E"), with calorie being the unit of measurement of energy. This means that one small gram of hydrogen would give 21 *trillion* units of energy!

A chocolate chip cookie contains 227 calories. If you eat a chocolate chip cookie, your body gets 227 units of energy. Your body needs energy to do things like ride a bike or row a boat. To get 21 trillion units of energy you would need to eat about 94 billion chocolate chip cookies!

Thermonuclear fusion is the process the Sun uses to convert hydrogen into helium and energy. With the tremendous amounts of energy thermonuclear fusion creates, the Sun can fuel our entire planet!

4.5 Summary

- The Moon is made of the same elements found on Earth.

- The Moon is smaller than the Earth with little or no atmosphere and no liquid water.

- The light areas of the Moon are called terrae and the dark areas are called maria.

- The Sun is a large celestial body composed mainly of the two gases, hydrogen and helium.

- The Sun converts hydrogen to helium and generates energy using thermonuclear fusion.

Chapter 5 Planets

5.1 Introduction

In the first four chapters we have been introduced to the Earth, the Moon, and the Sun. Although all of these celestial bodies are made of the same elements as those found on Earth, they also differ from each other in significant ways. We discovered that the Earth is a planet, the Moon is a moon, and the Sun is a star. In this chapter we will take a look at different types of planets.

5.2 Types of Planets

Each of the planets that orbits the Sun is unique. Earth is the only planet that has liquid water and an atmosphere that is breathable by humans. Jupiter is the only planet where immense storm systems last for centuries, and Venus has a cloud layer made of sulfuric acid.

In our solar system there are officially eight planets (Pluto lost its status as a planet, and we'll find out why in Section 5.5). The names of the eight planets that orbit our Sun are Mercury, Venus, Earth, Mars, Jupiter, Saturn, Uranus, and Neptune.

Although the planets differ greatly from one another, they can be placed into two broad categories: the terrestrial (tə-res'-trē-əl) planets (Earth-like) and the Jovian (jō'-vē-ən) planets (Jupiter-like).

The terrestrial planets differ from the Jovian planets in their physical properties and distance from the Sun. The terrestrial planets are all made of rocky materials and are relatively close to the Sun compared to the Jovian planets. The Jovian planets are made primarily of helium and hydrogen and are at greater distances from the Sun.

5.3 Earth-like Planets

The terrestrial planets include Mercury, Venus, Earth, and Mars. The word terrestrial comes from the Latin word *terra* which means "earth."

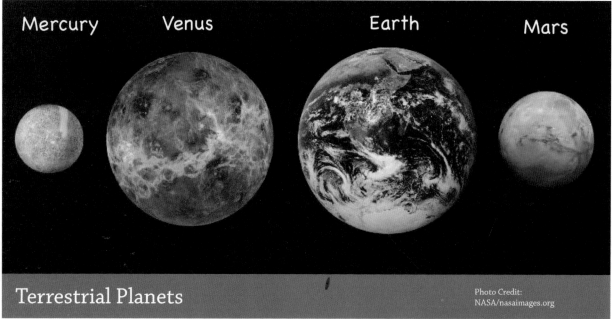

Mercury   Venus   Earth   Mars

Terrestrial Planets

Photo Credit:
NASA/nasaimages.org

All of the terrestrial planets resemble Earth in some ways. The terrestrial planets have hard, rocky surfaces with mountains, craters, and volcanoes.

Mercury is the terrestrial planet closest to the Sun. Because it is so close to the Sun, it is difficult to get images of it from Earth. However, in 1974 and 1975 an unmanned spacecraft called *Mariner 10* got close enough to Mercury to take photographs. The *Mariner 10* space probe revealed Mercury's rough, cratered surface. Although Mercury looks similar to the Moon, Mercury does not have the light and dark areas (terrae and maria) seen on the surface of the Moon.

Mercury
Photo Credit: NASA/nasaimages.org

CHAPTER 5: PLANETS 35

Venus is the next closest planet to orbit the Sun. Venus looks deceptively like Earth in size and shape. For years scientists thought Venus might be a warm jungle version of Earth with teeming life. But modern technologies have given us more information about Venus, and today we know that Venus is inhospitable for life.

The atmosphere on Venus is composed almost entirely of carbon dioxide. The high level of carbon dioxide creates a surface temperature of 460 degrees Celsius (860 degrees Fahrenheit).

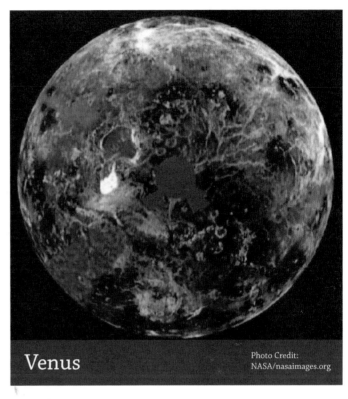

Venus

Photo Credit:
NASA/nasaimages.org

Mars

Photo Credit:
NASA/nasaimages.org

Also, the clouds that cover Venus contain corrosive sulfuric acid.

The fourth terrestrial planet from the Sun is Mars. People have been fascinated by Mars and have long speculated that life on Mars exists. "Martians" are a favorite character in many science fiction novels and films. Early astronomers even suggested that features on Mars included linear "canals," denoting intelligent life and liquid water. Today we know that Mars has no signs of life and no liquid water.

Mars is about half the diameter of Earth [6794 km (4220 mi)] with a relatively thin, almost cloudless atmosphere. Mars appears bright red to Earth observers, but the surface of Mars is actually reddish-brown. In the late 1960s several unmanned spacecraft flew past the surface of Mars. *Mariner 4, Mariner 6,* and *Mariner 7* sent back the first close-up pictures of the Martian surface and discovered that it is full of craters.

5.4 Jupiter-like Planets

The Jupiter-like, or Jovian, planets include Jupiter, Saturn, Uranus, and Neptune. The term Jovian comes from Roman mythological stories about Jove, who was the god of the sky. The Jovian planets are those planets that

Jovian Planets

Photo Credit:
NASA/nasaimages.org

resemble Jupiter in their physical properties and distance from the Sun. Jupiter is the largest of the Jovian planets, with a diameter about 11 times larger than that of the Earth. It is also about 318 times more massive. Jupiter orbits the Sun very slowly, taking almost 12 Earth years to make one orbit.

Looking at Jupiter through an Earth-based telescope, you can see light and dark bands circling the planetary surface. The light bands are called zones, and the dark bands are called belts. The zones and belts are parallel to Jupiter's equator and are colored red, orange, yellow, and brown. The zones and belts are gases at various temperatures. Scientists believe that the zones appear lighter because the clouds are higher and colder in this region, and the belts appear darker because the clouds are lower and warmer. The Great Red Spot

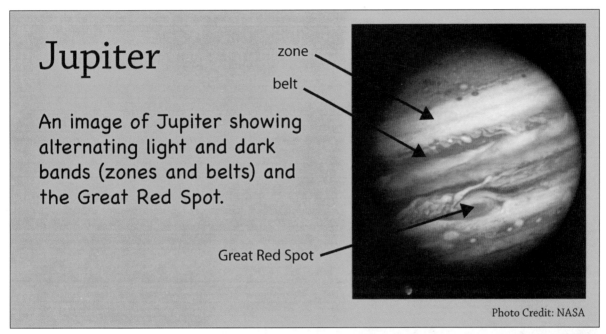

Jupiter

An image of Jupiter showing alternating light and dark bands (zones and belts) and the Great Red Spot.

zone

belt

Great Red Spot

Photo Credit: NASA

appears to be a huge long-lived storm where clouds complete a counterclockwise rotation about every six days. Jupiter is composed primarily of hydrogen and helium and has no rocky surface to break up the storm, so the storm has lasted for centuries.

Saturn is the next largest Jovian planet. With a diameter nearly

Saturn

Photo Credit:
NASA/nasaimages.org

9 times that of Earth, it is about 95 times more massive than Earth. Saturn, like Jupiter, is a mostly gaseous planet that slowly obits the Sun, taking 29 Earth years to make one orbit.

Like Jupiter, Saturn has belts and zones resulting from different gas clouds at different heights and temperatures. In addition to the belts and zones, Saturn has many colored rings extending laterally from the equator. Saturn's rings are believed to be made of many millions of icy fragments that are not connected but uniformly circle the planet. These icy fragments reflect the Sun's light, causing them to illuminate brightly.

The last of the Jovian planets are Uranus and Neptune. Uranus and Neptune extend to the darkest edge of our solar system and are many millions of miles away from the Sun.

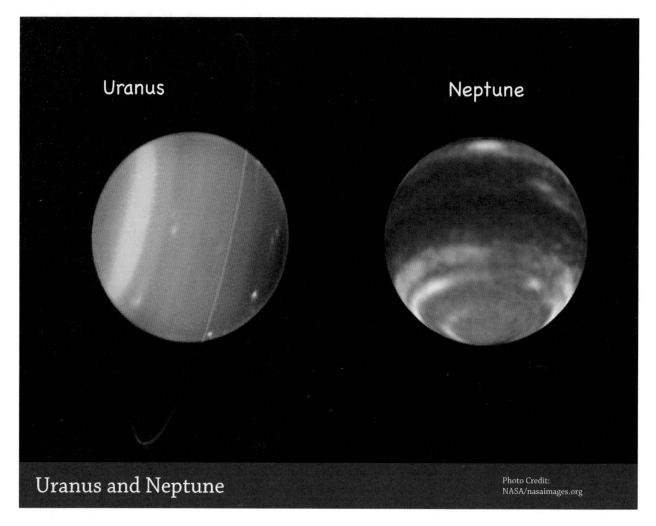

Uranus

Neptune

Uranus and Neptune

Photo Credit:
NASA/nasaimages.org

Uranus rotates around the Sun every 84 Earth years, is just over 4 times the diameter of Earth, and is 14 times as massive. Uranus has an almost featureless surface without zones and belts. Uranus is made up of mostly hydrogen and helium, like Jupiter and Saturn, but also contains a significant amount of methane. The presence of methane gives Uranus a distinctive bluish color. Computer imaging shows some very faint banding which is thought to be the result of sunlight breaking down the methane gas on the planet's surface. Uranus sits on its side as it orbits the Sun and, like Saturn, it is circled by several rings.

Uranus is colder than either Jupiter or Saturn. Because of its low temperature, Uranus does not have dense clouds like those of Jupiter and Saturn, and this may explain its very bland, featureless surface.

Neptune rotates around the Sun every 164 Earth years and like Uranus is about 4 times the diameter of Earth. But Neptune differs from Uranus in that it is 17 times more massive than Earth and has Jupiter-like atmospheric clouds, belts, and zones. In 1989 the unmanned spacecraft *Voyager 2* flew past Neptune and captured images of a giant storm called the Great Dark Spot. The Great Dark Spot was similar in many ways to Jupiter's Great Red Spot but was not as long-lived. In 1994 telescope images revealed that the storm had disappeared.

5.5 What Happened to Pluto?

Until recently Pluto was a favorite planet for many celestial enthusiasts, both young and old. Until August 2006 Pluto, at the far outer edge of our solar system, was considered the tiniest of the planets.

Pluto was discovered by Clyde Tombaugh on January 23, 1930. Tombaugh was troubled by what appeared to be irregularities in the orbits of both Uranus and Neptune. Many astronomers

Pluto—size comparison (diam.)

Image Credit: NASA/JPL-Caltech/R. Hurt (SSC)

of Tombaugh's day were troubled by the fact that Uranus and Neptune did not orbit the Sun as the astronomers thought they should. Tombaugh, knowing that neighboring planets can disturb planetary motions, found Pluto as a dim speck among the stars. Pluto was immediately given the title of the 9th planet in our solar system.

But, as it turns out, the naming of Pluto as a planet was a mistake. It was later determined that Pluto is too small to disturb the orbits of Uranus and Neptune. Also, astronomers decided there was nothing wrong with their orbits in the first place.

Solar System (as of 2006) with eight planets   Image Credit: International Astronomical Union (www.iau.org)

In 2006 the International Astronomers Union (IAU) had a meeting to discuss the definition of a planet. At this meeting it was decided that in order to qualify as a planet, a celestial body must have "cleared the neighborhood around its orbit." In other words, it can't have other celestial bodies orbiting the Sun with it. Pluto is actually in a belt of other celestial bodies called the Kuiper (kī'-pər) Belt. So the IAU reclassified Pluto as a dwarf planet rather than a true planet. A dwarf planet has not cleared its orbit but does have enough gravity to have formed a spherical shape like a true planet. However, as is typical in science, the debate continues. As of the writing of this text, the IAU has come up with a new classification for Pluto called a plutoid. A plutoid is like a dwarf planet but its orbit is beyond that of Neptune. Other scientists don't accept the IAU's definitions at all and would like to have Pluto reinstated as a planet. Who knows—a future young astronomer may help Pluto regain its planetary status!

5.6 Summary

● There are officially eight planets in our solar system: Mercury, Venus, Earth, Mars, Jupiter, Saturn, Uranus, and Neptune.

● The terrestrial planets are "earth-like" (made up of mostly rock) and are Mercury, Venus, Earth, and Mars.

● The Jovian planets are "Jupiter-like" (made up of mostly hydrogen and helium) and are Jupiter, Saturn, Uranus, and Neptune.

● Pluto was considered the 9th planet in the solar system, but lost its planetary status in 2006. It is now considered a dwarf planet or a plutoid.

Chapter 6 Our Solar System

ARE WE THERE YET?

ALMOST! ONLY 12.6 YEARS LEFT!

SUN 10,000,000 M

6.1 Introduction

In the last chapter we examined the eight planets of our solar system. We saw that the planets are divided into two broad categories: terrestrial planets and Jovian planets. We discovered that the terrestrial planets are mostly made of rock, like Earth, and the Jovian planets are mostly made of gases, like Jupiter.

In this chapter we will take a closer look at all of the planets together as a solar system. A solar system is a group of celestial bodies and the single sun they orbit. All of the planets we examined in the last chapter orbit a single sun, our Sun, and together are considered a "system."

6.2 Planetary Position

If we look at the entire system of planets, we see that the Sun is in the center of the solar system with the planets orbiting the Sun in a particular order. Mercury orbits closest to the Sun followed by Venus, Earth, Mars, Jupiter, Saturn, Uranus, and finally Neptune.

Because the distance from the Sun to the planets is very large, astronomers measure planetary distances in units called astronomical units, or AU. One AU is equal to 149,597,870.7 kilometers (92,955,801 miles). To get an idea of just how far one AU is, imagine that you had to drive from the Earth to the Sun (1 AU) in your car going 97 kilometers per hour (60 miles per hour). To get to the Sun this way, it would take 1,549,263 hours or 64,552 days, or about 177 years to get there!

Using AU to measure the distance of the planets from the Sun, you can see that the four terrestrial planets are relatively close together. All of the terrestrial planets are less than 2 AU from the Sun with Mercury the closest at 0.387 AU and Mars the farthest at 1.524 AU.

Planets and their distances from the Sun

Photo Credit:
NASA/nasaimages.org

In between the terrestrial planets and the Jovian planets is a huge 4 AU space. Jupiter, the closest of the Jovian planets, is 5.2 AU from the Sun, and Neptune, the farthest of the Jovian planets, is an incredibly far 30 AU from the Sun!

6.3 Planetary Orbits

An orbit is defined as the gravitational curved path of one celestial body moving around another celestial body. In other words, the orbit is the "road" a planet travels as it circles the Sun, and the Sun's gravity is what holds the planet in its orbit.

All of the planets orbit the Sun in a counterclockwise direction, and if we take a look straight down at the planetary orbits, we discover that the orbits look almost circular. They are not fully circular and so are technically elliptical, but they are not as elliptical as many people think they are.

One common misconception about Earth's seasons is that the Earth's orbit gives us the summer and winter months. However, by examining Earth's orbit it is easy to see that the difference between Earth's farthest and closest distance from the Sun is very small. In other words, Earth does not move significantly far away from the Sun. As we discussed in Chapter 3, the seasons are determined by Earth's tilt on its axis, *not its distance from the Sun*. The Earth tilts toward the Sun in the summer months and away from the Sun in the winter months.

The terrestrial planets compose the inner solar system, and the Jovian planets make up the outer solar system. Recall from Section 6.2 that there is a large gap between Mars and Jupiter.

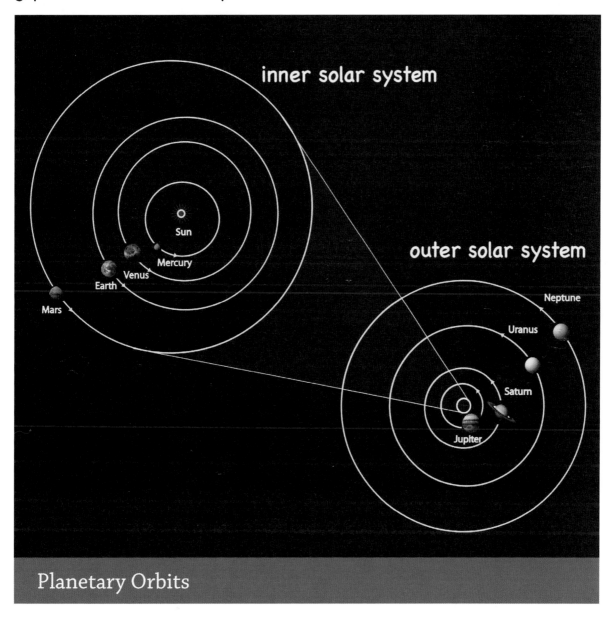

Planetary Orbits

6.4 Asteroids, Meteorites, and Comets

The gap between Mars and Jupiter is not empty space but is home to millions of asteroids. The word asteroid comes from the Greek word *aster* which means "star." When asteroids are viewed in the sky, they resemble small stars. An asteroid is not a real star like our Sun, but instead is a small celestial body made mostly of rock and minerals. The asteroids between Mars and Jupiter occupy what is known as the Asteroid Belt.

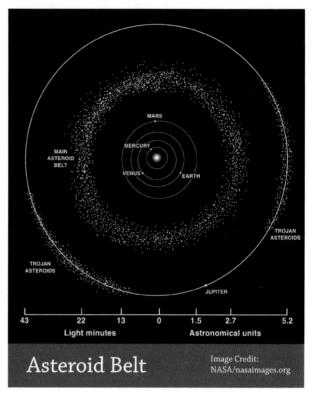

Asteroid Belt

Image Credit: NASA/nasaimages.org

Today there are more than 50,000 known asteroids. Most asteroids are smaller than 1 km (.62 mi) in diameter, but a few are much larger, like Asteroid Lutetia which is 100 km (62 mi) wide. Asteroids often have irregular shapes. Asteroid Gaspra is an asteroid with an elongated body, and Asteroid Kleopatra has a dog bone shape.

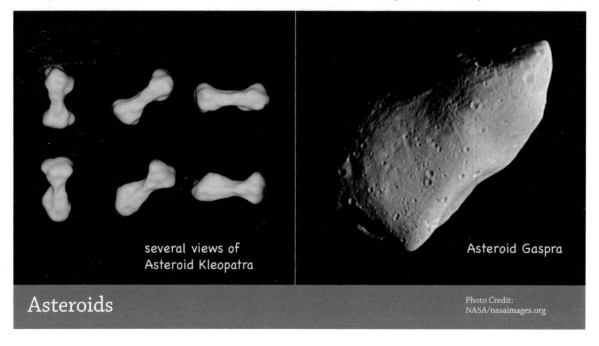

several views of
Asteroid Kleopatra

Asteroid Gaspra

Asteroids

Photo Credit:
NASA/nasaimages.org

Although there are great distances between asteroids in the Asteroid Belt, asteroids sometimes collide. Because asteroids are moving at great speeds, when they collide, they impact at speeds more than sufficient to shatter rock. Many asteroids show craters on their surfaces as a result of these high impact collisions.

Asteroids are also found outside the Asteroid Belt and do occasionally impact Earth. Small asteroids, if they cross into the Earth's atmosphere, are called meteors. They often break up into smaller pieces and burn up before reaching the surface of the Earth. Meteors that reach the Earth's surface are called meteorites. Depending on their composition, meteorites are called "stones" or "stony irons."

A comet is another type of celestial body found in our solar system. Comets are large chucks of dirty ice. Occasionally the orbit of a comet will bring it close to the Sun. When this happens, the Sun's heat vaporizes some of the ice, changing the water from its solid state to a gas and creating long tails of gas and dust particles.

Halley's Comet

Hale-Bopp Comet

Comets

Photo Credit:
NASA/nasaimages.org

There are several famous comets that have been photographed in the last few decades. In 1986 Halley's Comet passed close enough to Earth for several spacecraft to gather information about it.

Halley's Comet has a potato-shaped center about 15 kilometers (9 miles) long and a long tail made of various frozen gases such as carbon dioxide, methane, and ammonia. In 1997 Hale-Bopp Comet passed by Earth, displaying a beautiful fluorescent blue-white tail made of ionized carbon monoxide molecules.

6.5 Habitable Earth

Within our solar system, as far as we know, there are no other planets, moons, or other celestial bodies that can support life as we know it. Scientists have long been searching for other planets like Earth that could be home to alien life. But so far, science fiction novels are the only place aliens exist.

What makes Earth uniquely habitable?

One unique feature of Earth is our atmosphere. Our transparent atmosphere helps maintain the necessary balance of water, gas, and energy. No other atmosphere like Earth's is known to exist.

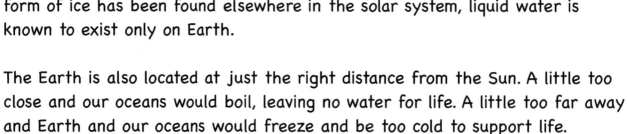

All known life is dependent on liquid water, and although water in the form of ice has been found elsewhere in the solar system, liquid water is known to exist only on Earth.

The Earth is also located at just the right distance from the Sun. A little too close and our oceans would boil, leaving no water for life. A little too far away and Earth and our oceans would freeze and be too cold to support life.

Finally, the Moon stabilizes Earth's tilt, and the large planets, Jupiter and Saturn, actually shield the inner solar system from too much impact by comets. So both the Moon and the planets help stabilize Earth's habitability.

6.6 Summary

- The terrestrial planets (Mercury, Venus, Earth, and Mars) make up the inner solar system and are "close" to the Sun (less than 2 AU).

- The Jovian planets (Jupiter, Saturn, Uranus, and Neptune) make up the outer solar system, and are "far" from the Sun (more than 5 AU from the Sun).

- Each of the eight planets has a slightly elliptical orbit (very close to circular).

- Asteroids exist throughout the solar system, but most asteroids are found in The Asteroid Belt between Mars and Jupiter.

- The Earth is the only known habitable celestial body in our solar system and is uniquely suited for life.

Chapter 7 Other Solar Systems

Lalande 21185
Wolf 359
Barnard's
Sun
Alpha Centauri
Complex

Alpha Centauri
System
Proxima Centauri
270,000 AU
Our Solar System

7.1 Introduction

In Chapters 5 and 6 we explored the planets and our solar system. We saw that the Sun is the center of our solar system, and the planets orbit the Sun in a counterclockwise direction. We discovered that Earth is unique among the planets in our solar system in that it is the only planet that we know to support life. But what about planets in other solar systems? Are there other suns in our universe that have planets orbiting them? Do any of these other solar systems support life? In this chapter we will explore some of our nearest solar neighbors.

7.2 Closest Stars

If we look outside our solar system and beyond our Sun, we discover that there are other stars and solar systems. The closest stars to our solar system are actually part of a triple-star system called the Alpha Centauri (sen-tô'-rē) system.

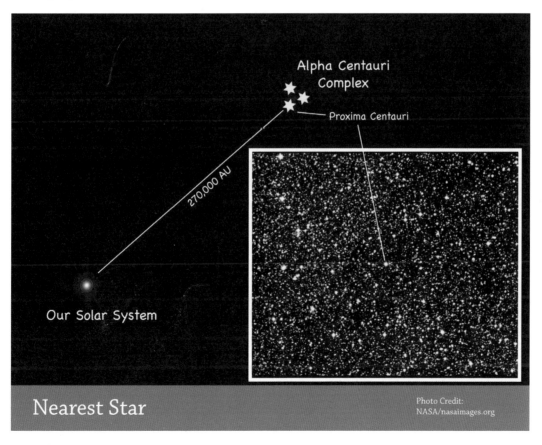

The three stars in this triple-star system are bound together by gravity, and they orbit each other. Two of these stars are similar to our Sun and are called Alpha Centauri A and Alpha Centauri B. The third star is called Proxima Centauri, and it is the star that is closest to Earth.

Even though Proxima Centauri is closest to our solar system, it is still about 270,000 AU away. This means that the distance from Earth to Proxima Centauri is almost 300,000 times the distance from Earth to our Sun!

The next nearest stars to our solar system are Barnard's Star, Lalande 21185, and Wolf 359. All of these stars are many millions of miles away from our solar system.

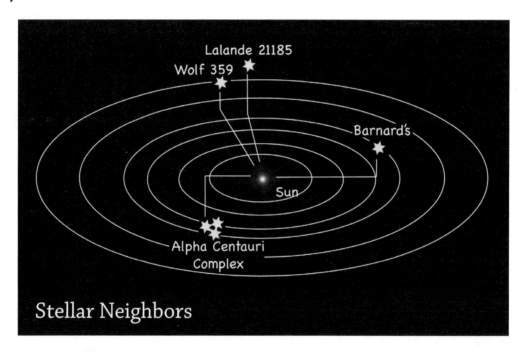

Because stellar distances are extremely large, astronomers measure these distances in parsecs. We saw in Chapter 6 that Earth is 1 AU from the Sun, which is about 150 million kilometers (93 million miles). A parsec is equal to 206,260 AUs or about 19,000,000,000,000 miles! It is easy to see why astronomers measure stellar distances in parsecs.

Barnard's Star is roughly 1.1 parsecs from Earth, Lalande 21185 is 1.4 parsecs from Earth, and Wolf 359 is about 2.4 parsecs from Earth.

7.3 Constellations

When you look up at the night sky, you can see many stars. The stars are often associated with groups called constellations. Constellations are patterns of stars ancient astronomers named after mythological heros or animals.

It is interesting to note that ancient astronomers from different cultures often grouped the same stars together in the same constellations. A group of seven stars known as the "Big Dipper" in North America was known by the ancient Greeks as "the Great Bear." This same group is called "The Plough" or "Wagon" in western Europe and "The Stag" by ancient Siberians. The Egyptians saw this group of stars as the "leg of an ox."

Some common constellations include Canis Major, "The Big Dog," and Orion, "The Hunter." It is possible to study the stars and how they move by observing the constellations. Many people from both modern and ancient times have studied the stars and their constellations. Modern astronomers also use references to constellations when discussing the positions of stars.

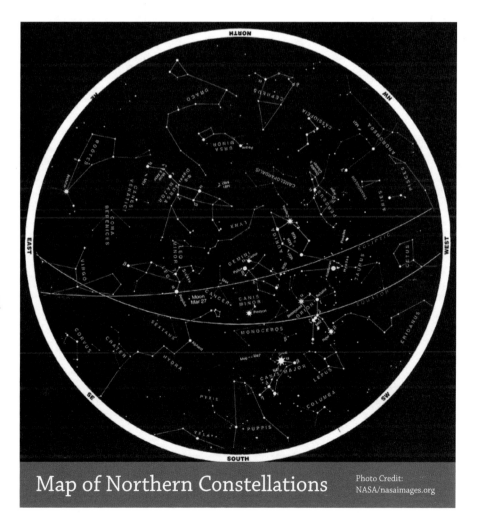

Map of Northern Constellations

Photo Credit:
NASA/nasaimages.org

7.4 Brightest and Largest Stars

The brightest stars in the sky are not necessarily the closest or largest stars. Sirius is the brightest star in the sky, but it is 2.6 parsecs away from our Sun. It is not as close as the Alpha Centauri star system. But Sirius is 20 times brighter than our Sun and over twice as large.

Sirius can be found in the Canis Major constellation. Sirius has a secondary star associated with it called Sirius B which is significantly dimmer than Sirius.

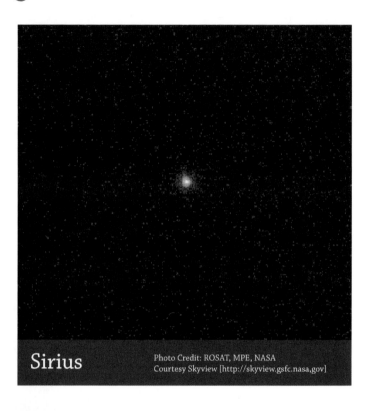

Sirius

Photo Credit: ROSAT, MPE, NASA
Courtesy Skyview [http://skyview.gsfc.nasa.gov]

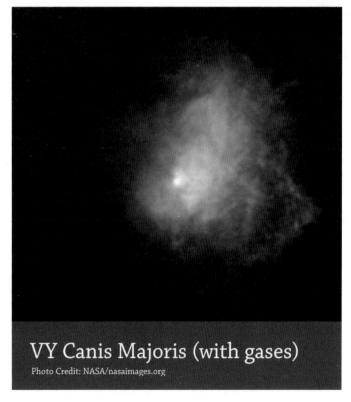

VY Canis Majoris (with gases)

Photo Credit: NASA/nasaimages.org

The largest star visible in the night sky is the star VY Canis Majoris (VY CMa). This star dwarfs our Sun by several magnitudes. A magnitude is the measurement of the brightness of a celestial body.

VY Canis Majoris is considered a red hypergiant star and is located in the constellation Canis Major. VY CMa is very far away from our Sun at a distance of 1500 parsecs. It is a solitary star and does not have multiple stars associated with it. VY CMa is a very active star that emits large amounts of gas during stellar outbursts, which are eruptions of electrically charged particles from a star's surface. These stellar outbursts result in mass being ejected from the star.

7.5 Planets Near Other Stars

Because the large amount of light generated by a star hides the much smaller planets that lie close to the star, it has been difficult to confirm the existence of extrasolar planets. Extrasolar planets (or exoplanets) are planets that orbit stars outside our solar system. Exoplanets have been discussed since the middle of the 20th century, but it wasn't until 1994 that the existence of planets outside our solar system was confirmed.

Exoplanets as seen by the Hubble telescope

Photo Credit: NASA/nasaimages.org

In March 2009 NASA launched the Kepler space telescope with the mission of finding Earth-size and smaller planets around other stars in the Milky Way Galaxy (the large group of stars that contains our solar system). The Kepler space telescope is in orbit around the Sun and is named after Johannes Kepler (1571-1630), the German astronomer who developed the laws of planetary motion to describe how the planets move around the Sun.

Using data sent to Earth from the Kepler space telescope, astronomers have been able to confirm the existence of exoplanets and also to estimate how many exoplanets may be in our galaxy. Scientists

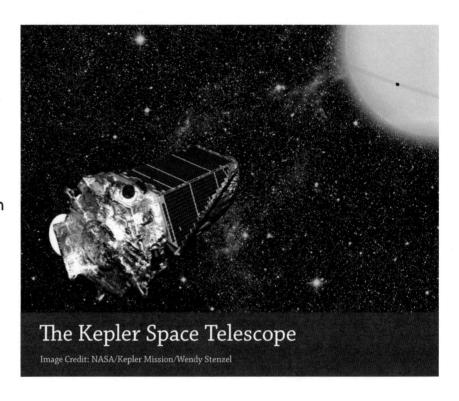

The Kepler Space Telescope
Image Credit: NASA/Kepler Mission/Wendy Stenzel

now think that in our galaxy alone there may be billions of planets that are of a size similar to that of Earth, and the total number of planets may be hundreds of billions.

Astronomers classify exoplanets according to their Jupiter-like or Earth-like characteristics. There are massive Jovian-type planets referred to as Jupiters and less massive Jovian planets called Neptunes. There are also planets whose masses are up to 10 times that of Earth, and these are referred to as super-Earths. Exoplanets also differ depending on how far they are from their parent sun. Planets that orbit close to their sun are called hot planets and have extremely high temperatures, while planets farther away are called cold planets due to their colder temperatures.

7.6 The Circumstellar Habitable Zone

Today we know that planetary systems are common in the universe. In order for an exoplanet to support life as we know it, the planet would have to be found in a particular area of its solar system called the Circumstellar Habitable Zone. In this region, an Earth-like planet would be neither too hot nor too cold and would maintain liquid water.

This habitable zone is like a three dimensional shell that surrounds any given star. For small stars, the habitable zone is close to the star, and for larger stars the habitable zone is farther away. Although there may be billions of planets in habitable zones in the Milky Way Galaxy, it is not known whether any of them have the right conditions for life as we know it.

7.7 Summary

- Proxima Centauri in the Alpha Centauri system is our nearest stellar neighbor.

- The distances of stars are measured in parsecs. One parsec equals 206,260 AUs.

- Early astronomers grouped stars into patterns called constellations. Modern astronomers still use the names of constellations to discuss star positions.

- The stars that appear brightest and largest from Earth are not the closest stars.

- Extrasolar planets, also called exoplanets, are planets that orbit stars outside our solar system. Many stars are confirmed as having exoplanets.

- Earth is situated in an area called the Circumstellar Habitable Zone.

Chapter 8 Our Galaxy

8.1 Introduction

In Chapter 7 we looked at stars outside our solar system. We discovered that stars can be very large and very bright. We also discovered that exoplanets orbit other stars, creating other solar systems.

Where do these other solar systems live? Are they close to Earth or far away? Are they held together in a group or are they spread out? As we move away from our solar system and farther into space is there anything special about where we and our neighboring solar systems reside?

In this chapter we will explore these questions and others as we look at the area of the universe that we call our galaxy.

8.2 The Milky Way

A galaxy (ga'-lək-sē) is a large collection of stars, gas, dust, planets, and other objects held together by its own gravity. The Milky Way Galaxy is the galaxy that our Earth, Sun, and solar system occupy.

We cannot observe the entire Milky Way Galaxy because Earth is in the midst of its vast area and occupies just one small piece of it. Since we live inside the galaxy, it is challenging to uncover its nature. We might compare the effort to map our own galaxy to a scuba diver trying to map the entire ocean. It is easier to gather significant details about other galaxies because we can see the whole galaxy from the outside. Studying other galaxies helps us to understand more about our own.

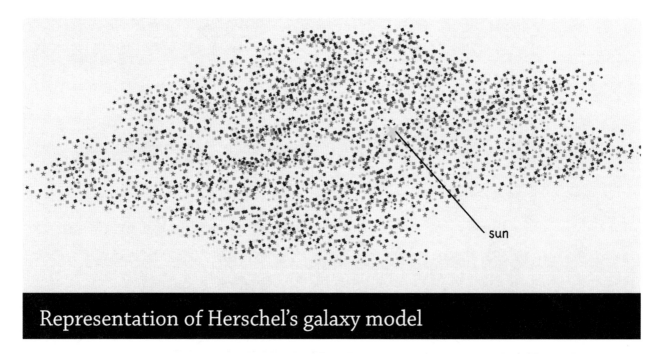

sun

Representation of Herschel's galaxy model

Early astronomers had very different ideas about the size, shape, and nature of our galaxy than we do now. In 1785 the English astronomer William Herschel presented a paper with his conclusions about the size and shape of our galaxy. Hershel counted as many stars as he could in each direction, and from this data he created a map that he thought represented our galaxy. Hershel's map showed the Milky Way as a flat, disk-shaped collection of stars, with our Sun at or near the center.

8.3 Shape and Size

Today we know that galaxies come in many shapes and sizes. Astronomers group the many variations they see into three basic types of galaxies, called spirals, ellipticals, and irregulars. (We will learn more about other galaxies in Chapter 9.)

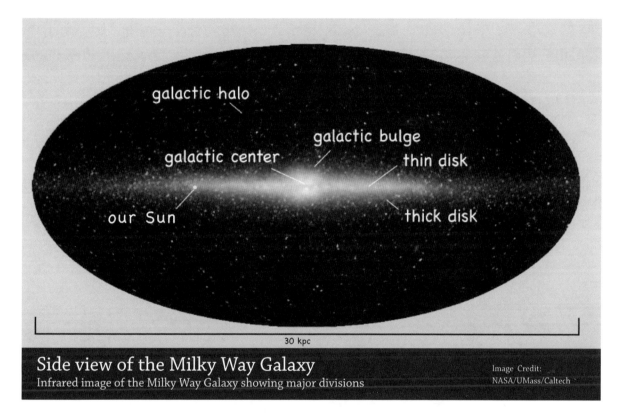

Side view of the Milky Way Galaxy
Infrared image of the Milky Way Galaxy showing major divisions

Image Credit:
NASA/UMass/Caltech

We now know that our galaxy is not entirely flat nor is the Sun at the center. Modern astronomers have observed that the Milky Way Galaxy is a type called a spiral galaxy. If we could take a spaceship outside our galaxy and take a picture from the top, we would likely see that our galaxy has spiral arms similar to a pinwheel. It also has a central bulge from which the spiral arms extend.

The Milky Way Galaxy can be divided into four regions. The galactic bulge (also called the central bulge) is a dense ball of old stars at the center of the galaxy. The thin disk orbits the galactic bulge, contains the majority of the stars, and looks almost circular when viewed from above. The younger and more massive stars are found here, and new stars are formed in this area. The thin disk is the part of the Milky Way that we see at night as a faint band of light in the sky. The thick disk surrounds the thin disk and contains older stars. Surrounding the galaxy is the galactic halo, a spherical group of very old stars and gas. Our Sun and Earth are located in the thin disk, and astronomers believe that our solar system is about two-thirds of the way from the galactic bulge to the edge of the galaxy.

Radio studies have provided enough information for astronomers to reach the conclusion that the Milky Way Galaxy has a spiral shape. The spiraling arms start in the center of the Galaxy at the galactic bulge and extend outward. Recently, astronomers have concluded that there are two major spiral arms, Scutum-Centaurus (scü'-təm sen-tô'-rəs) and Perseus (pər'-süs or pər'-sē-əs), and two minor arms, the Norma Arm and the Sagittarius (sa-jə-ter'-ē-əs) Arm. Earth resides on a small, partial spiral arm called the Orion Arm that is in between the Sagittarius Arm and the Perseus Arm.

Artist's view of the Milky Way as it might appear from above
Image Credit: NASA/JPL-Caltech

How big is the Milky Way Galaxy? Since we are on a small planet circling a relatively small sun off to one side of a huge galaxy, it's tough to measure its size. Because we can't take a space ship and a yardstick to the end of the galaxy, astronomers estimate distances by using other techniques. Early astronomers assumed that all stars are equally bright and used this assumption to estimate that the diameter of our Milky Way Galaxy is around 10 kiloparsecs (kpc), with one kpc being equal to 1,000 parsecs. Today, astronomers believe that our galaxy is at least 30 kpc in diameter.

Milky Way Galaxy center

Photo Credit: NASA/JPL-Caltech/S. Stolovy (Spitzer Science Center/Caltech)

In the early 20th century an American astronomer named Harlow Shapley figured out a way to use variable stars to get a more accurate measurement of a galaxy's size. A variable, or pulsating, star is a star whose luminosity changes with time. A full description of how astronomers measure distances using pulsating stars is beyond the scope of this text, but basically astronomers calculate distances by use of a mathematical relationship between the luminosity of the star and the star's apparent brightness.

$$\text{apparent brightness} = \text{luminosity}/\text{distance}^2$$

8.4 Galactic Habitable Zone

In Chapter 7 we saw that Earth resides in an area of space called the Circumstellar Habitable Zone, which is the area near a star where conditions are "just right" for the existence of life as we know it.

The same is true for a solar system in a galaxy. Our solar system is located in the galactic habitable zone, just the "right" place in the Milky Way Galaxy for life as we know it to exist. If our solar system were too far from the galactic center, there might not be enough heavy elements for a terrestrial planet like Earth to form. If our solar system were too close to the galactic center, there might be unfavorable levels of radiation or gravity for life as we know it to form. So Earth seems to be located at just the right place in the galaxy.

sun

Galactic Habitable Zone

8.5 Summary

● A galaxy is a large collection of stars, gas, dust, planets and other objects held together by its own gravity.

● The Milky Way Galaxy is a spiral shaped galaxy with a galactic bulge at the center of a thin disk.

● The size of the Milky Way Galaxy is estimated to be 30 kiloparsecs (kpc).

● Earth resides between the Sagittarius Arm and the Perseus Arm on a small, partial spiral arm called the Orion Arm.

● Our solar system is situated in an area called the galactic habitable zone.

Chapter 9 Other Galaxies

9.1 Introduction

In Chapter 8 we looked closely at our home galaxy, the Milky Way Galaxy. We discovered that the Milky Way Galaxy is a spiral galaxy with a bulge in the center of an almost circular thin disk of stars.

But what about other galaxies? Are there other spiral galaxies similar to ours? What other shapes do galaxies form? How large are other galaxies and how many stars might they hold? How many galaxies are there?

10,000 Galaxies

Image credit: NASA, ESA, S. Beckwith (STSci), and the HUDF Team

In this chapter we will look at a few different galaxy types. Galaxies are classified by how they look. The four major types of galaxies are: spiral galaxies, barred spiral galaxies, elliptical galaxies, and irregular galaxies.

The astronomer responsible for these galaxy categories is Edwin Hubble. Although there are other classification schemes, the Hubble classification, which was developed in 1936, is still used today to sort the variety of galaxies observed by astronomers.

9.2 Spiral Galaxies

As we saw in Chapter 8, the Milky Way Galaxy looks like a pinwheel with a bulge in the middle and arms radiating from it. This type of galaxy is called a spiral galaxy.

All spiral galaxies are similar in shape, with a flattened galactic disk and spiral arms extending from the middle. All spiral galaxies have a galactic bulge in the center and an extended galactic halo. In Hubble's classification scheme, spiral galaxies are given the letter S and subdivided further by the size of the galactic bulge using the letters a, b, and c. Sa galaxies have the largest galactic bulge and Sc the smallest.

The nearest spiral galaxy to our own is the Andromeda (an-drä'-mə-də) Galaxy. The Andromeda Galaxy is also known as Messier 31, M31, or NGC 224, and is classified as an Sb galaxy. The Andromeda Galaxy is found in the constellation Andromeda, and this is where it gets its name.

Andromeda Galaxy

Image credit:
NASA/JPL-Caltech/K. Gordon (University of Arizona)

Another spiral galaxy found by astronomers is Messier 81 (M81). M81 is an Sb galaxy that is tilted with respect to our galaxy. As a result, we can get a particularly nice view of the galactic bulge and spiral arms. M81 is one of the brightest galaxies in the sky and is found in the Ursa Major constellation.

Messier 81 (M81) Galaxy

Image credit: NASA/JPL-Caltech/S. Wilmer
(Harvard-Smithsonian Center for Astrophysics)

9.3 Barred Spiral Galaxies

The second category of galaxies created by Hubble is the barred spiral galaxy. A barred spiral galaxy is similar to a spiral galaxy except that the spiral arms originate at the ends of a bar-shaped region that goes through the center of the galaxy's galactic bulge. Barred spiral galaxies are designated by the letters SB and further subdivided with the letters a, b, and c depending on the size of the galactic bulge. Sometimes astronomers cannot distinguish between spiral galaxies and barred spiral galaxies. This is especially true when the galaxy is edge-on toward Earth, and we can only see the galaxy from the side and not the top. The Milky Way Galaxy is now thought have an elongated bar in the center and is probably a barred spiral galaxy rather than a regular spiral galaxy. However, the size of the bar remains uncertain.

Barred Spiral Galaxy NGC 1365

Image credit:
NASA/JPL-Caltech/SSC

9.4 Elliptical Galaxies

Elliptical galaxies are different from both spiral galaxies and barred spiral galaxies in that they have no spiral arms or internal features such as a galactic bulge. Elliptical galaxies are ellipse-shaped congregates of stars with the density of stars increasing toward the center. Elliptical galaxies are denoted by the letter "E" and subdivided further with a number from 0 to 7. An elliptical galaxy classified as E0 is nearly circular, and an elliptical galaxy designated E7 is the most elongated of this group.

Two Elliptical Galaxies NGC 0533 and NGC 5044
Image credit: X-ray—NASA/CXC/U Ohio/T. Statler & S. Diehl; Optical—DSS

9.5 Irregular Galaxies

The final class of galaxies identified by Hubble are those galaxies referred to as irregular galaxies. This is a broad term that describes all of those galaxies that don't seem to fit into the other categories. Irregular galaxies aren't really spiral, although they may have an arm or two. They aren't really elliptical but can be circular or elongated. Irregulars don't really have a galactic bulge in the center, but they can have a high density of stars off to one side.

The Irregular Galaxy AM 0644-741

Image credit: NASA/NASA Hubble Space Telescope Collection

9.6 Summary

● The Hubble classification scheme for galaxies divides galaxies into four major groups: spiral, barred spiral, elliptical, and irregular.

● Spiral and barred spiral galaxies both have spiral arms extending from a galactic bulge. In the case of barred spiral galaxies, the galactic bulge is elongated.

● Elliptical galaxies are either circular or elongated.

● Irregular galaxies have no defined shape.

Chapter 10 The Universe

10.1 Introduction

In Chapter 9 we explored other galaxies. We saw that there are different types of galaxies with different features. Some galaxies are like our Milky Way Galaxy with spiral arms and a galactic bulge. Some galaxies are simply circular or elliptical without arms. And some galaxies are completely irregular and don't fit into any of the other categories.

What else is in space? Are there only galaxies, stars, and planets? Are there other types of objects in deep space that astronomers have observed? What happens when stars run out of fuel? Do they explode or find other ways to create light? What about the universe as whole? What other interesting features can be found in our universe?

In this chapter we will explore a few interesting features of the universe, like red giants, novae, supernovae, black holes, and nebulae.

10.2 Red Giants and White Dwarfs

Will the Sun always burn with the same intensity that it burns with today? What happens to stars like our Sun as they get old or run out of fuel? Does the star find ways to make other fuel, or does it just get too old to continue?

No one really knows for sure how stars begin and how they end because no one was around to observe the beginning of stars. Yet, because there are so many stars in the universe, astronomers can get an idea of how stars age by looking at stars that are at different stages. Just as a person studying humans might look at people at all different stages in life to get an idea of how they grow and change, astronomers look at different stars to develop theories about how stars change.

Recall from Chapter 4 that stars create light and heat energy in a process called thermonuclear fusion. During this process, hydrogen atoms are fused to create helium. The hydrogen used by stars for thermonuclear fusion can't last forever, and eventually the hydrogen is used up by the star. At this point the star begins to collapse, putting more pressure on the core and causing the temperature to rise. When the pressure and temperature are high enough, the star begins to fuse helium. When this happens, there is actually more thermonuclear fusion created in the star, and the star gets hotter, bigger, and brighter. The star becomes a red giant star.

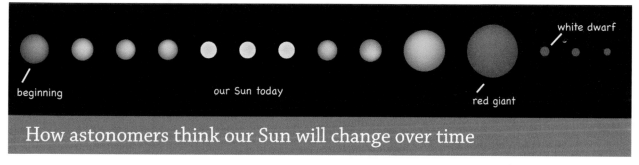

white dwarf

beginning

our Sun today

red giant

How astonomers think our Sun will change over time

After the star becomes a red giant, it is burning hotter and brighter, making it extremely unstable. This unstable star is rapidly burning more and more fuel. Eventually, when it has finally used all of the fuel it has, the star burns out, leaving only its core of nonburnable elements. When this happens, the star shrinks, becoming a white dwarf star.

10.3 Novae and Supernovae

Both novae (nō'-vē) and supernovae are stars that suddenly increase in brightness. A nova (nō'-və) will increase in brightness and then suddenly fade back to its original luminosity. A nova can cycle many times, brightening and then fading back to its original luminosity then going back to bright again. The word *nova* comes from Latin and means "new." To early astronomers who could only see these stars when they were bright, they appeared to be new stars. Today we know that novae are not new stars at all, but old stars that have become white dwarf stars. The white dwarfs undergo explosions on their surface that create variable brightness.

To fuel their bursts of light, novae acquire hydrogen from nearby stars. In this way a nova can cycle many times. The nova takes hydrogen to use for thermonuclear fusion, becoming bright. Then as the hydrogen is consumed, the nova's intensity fades.

A supernova is different from a nova. A supernova is an exploding star whose intensity suddenly increases and then slowly dims, eventually fading entirely

Feb. '94   Sept '94   Mar. '95   Feb '96

Supernova 1987A explosion debris
Image credit: January 14, 1997, Chun Shing Jason Pun (NASA/GSFC), Robert P. Kirshner (Harvard-Smithsonian Center for Astrophysics), and NASA

from view. As a supernova explodes into stellar debris, it produces light that is billions of times brighter than our Sun. In the image shown, astronomers using the Hubble telescope observed the changing luminosity of the Supernova 1987A.

10.4 Black Holes and Nebulae

Black holes have been a favorite in science fiction novels and in Hollywood, but do black holes actually exist? Scientists believe that when a very large star undergoes a supernova explosion, the collapse of the star's core due to gravity causes the protons and electrons in the core to combine to form neutrons. The result is a very dense neutron star. Scientists believe that when the neutron star later collapses, it creates a black hole. Black holes, neutron stars, and white dwarf stars are also referred to as stellar remnants.

Illustration of a black hole

Image credit:
NASA/CXC/M. Weiss

A black hole is believed to be an area in space from which no light can escape. Scientists believe that this can happen when a very large amount of solar mass, such as a neutron star, occupies a very small area of space. The solar mass is so compact (dense) in this area that nothing can escape its extreme gravity, not even a beam of light or an x-ray! These areas are called black holes.

Crab Nebula

Image credit:
NASA/ESA/JPL/Arizona State University

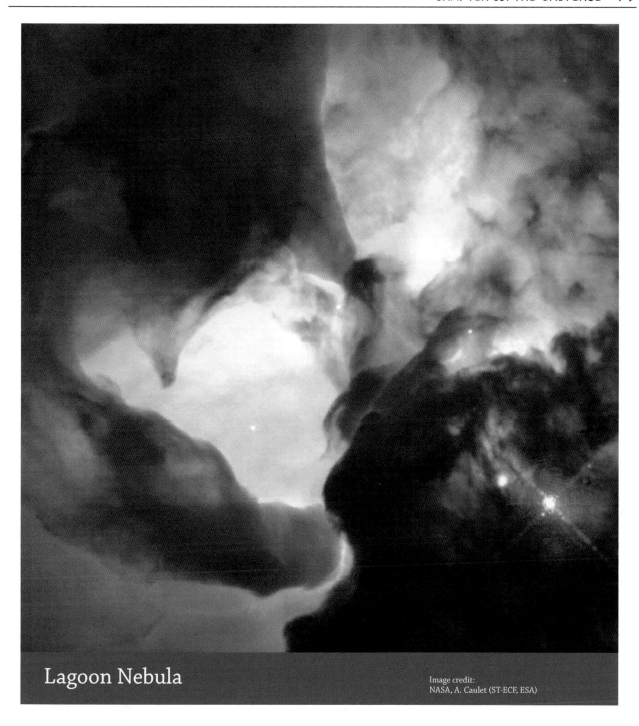

Lagoon Nebula

Image credit:
NASA, A. Caulet (ST-ECF, ESA)

There are several different kinds of nebulae (ne'-byə-lē). The word nebula (ne'-byə-lə) comes from the Latin word for "cloud," so nebula refers to any fuzzy patch of dust, hydrogen, helium, ionized matter, and other gases observed in interstellar space (among the stars).

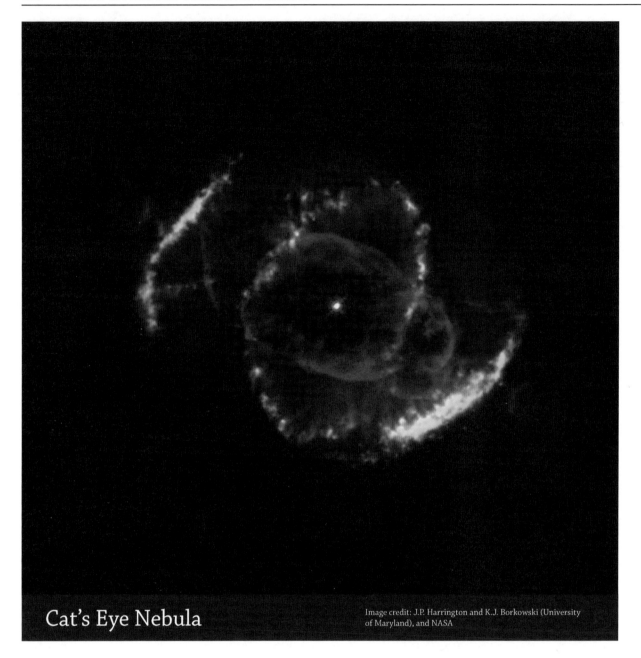

Cat's Eye Nebula

Image credit: J.P. Harrington and K.J. Borkowski (University of Maryland), and NASA

Some of the most spectacular deep space images come from emission nebulae. Emission nebulae are glowing clouds of interstellar matter made primarily of dust and ionized gases.

Nebulae also occur when a supernova collapses and ultraviolet radiation ionizes the surrounding area. These nebulae are called planetary nebulae. A planetary nebula displays a beautiful ring that surrounds the dense core of the star. So far, there are more than 3,000 planetary nebulae known in our galaxy.

10.5 A Universe We Can Discover

Humans have been studying the cosmos for centuries. The earliest astronomers gazed up at the sky, and with very little technological help, learned a great deal about our Sun, the planets in our solar system, and the stars in our galaxy. Today with the aid of advanced telescopes and computer technology, astronomers have gathered an enormous amount of data about the universe.

Earth is situated at just the right place in our solar system and at just the right place in our galaxy with just the right atmosphere for us to exist and to be able to gaze into clear skies and observe the remarkable objects dancing in our universe. The universe is vast and mysterious with many questions still unanswered. Yet, because humans are so curious about what lies beyond the horizon, new discoveries about the universe are constantly being made by both trained scientists and backyard hobbyists.

10.6 Summary

● A red giant is a star that has become larger, brighter, and hotter as it begins to burn helium for fuel.

● A white dwarf is a star that has used up all of its own fuel leaving just the core.

● Novae are stars that increase in luminosity, fade, and become bright again.

● A supernova is a star that suddenly increases in luminosity as it explodes, and then it slowly fades.

● A black hole is believed to occur when a large amount of mass left by a supernova occupies a small amount of space.

● Nebulae are clouds of dust, gases and ionized matter.

Glossary-Index

AU ● see astronomical unit

Alpha Centauri A (al'-fə sen-tô'-rē ā) ● a star that is similar to our Sun and is in the Alpha Centauri system; one of the stars closest to our solar system, 52

Alpha Centauri B (al'-fə sen-tô'-rē bē) ● a star that is similar to our Sun and is in the Alpha Centauri system; one of the stars closest to our solar system, 52

Alpha Centauri system (al'-fə sen-tô'-rē sis'-təm) ● a triple-star system that contains the stars closest to our solar system; Alpha Centauri A, Alpha Centauri B, and Proxima Centauri, 51-52, 57

Andromeda Galaxy (an-drä'-mə-də ga'-lək-sē) ● the nearest spiral galaxy to our Milky Way Galaxy; found in the constellation Andromeda; also called Messier 31, M31, or NGC 224, 68

Aristarchus of Samos (a-rə-stär'-kəs) (sā'-məs) ● (310-230 BC [BCE]) Greek astronomer and mathematician; believed in a heliocentric cosmos, 6, 7

Aristotle (a'-rə-stä-təl) ● Greek philosopher (384-322 BC [BCE]); studied motion and other physical laws, 6, 7

arms ● see spiral arms

asteroid (as'-tə-roid) ● [*aster*, Gr., star] a small, irregularly shaped celestial body made mostly of rock and minerals, 46-47, 49

Asteroid Belt ● a region between Mars and Jupiter that contains numerous asteroids, 46-47, 49

Asteroid Gaspra (gä'-sprə) ● an asteroid with an elongated body, 46-47

Asteroid Kleopatra (klē-ə-pa'-trə) ● a dog bone shaped asteroid, 46-47

Asteroid Lutetia (lü-tē'-shə) ● a very large asteroid that is 100 km wide, 46

astronomer (ə-strä'-nə-mər) ● [*aster*, Gr., star; *nomas*, Gr., to assign, distribute, or arrange] a scientist who assigns names to the celestial bodies, including stars, and studies how they exist and move in space, 2, 7

astronomical (as-trə-nä'-mi-kəl) **unit (AU)** ● a unit of measure used by astronomers; one AU is equal to 149,597,870.7 kilometers or 92,955,801 miles, the distance of the Earth from the Sun, 43-44, 49, 52, 57

astronomy (ə-strä'-nə-mē) ● [*aster*, Gr., star; *nomas*, Gr., to assign, distribute, or arrange] the study of the stars and other objects in space, 2, 7

atmosphere (at'-mə-sfir) ● [*atmos*, Gr., vapor] the gaseous layer surrounding a celestial body; the air surrounding the Earth, 12, 22, 26, 27, 48

atmospheric turbulence (at-mə-sfir'-ik tər'-byə-ləns) ● a disturbance of particles in the atmosphere, 12

atom (a'-təm) ● one of over 100 fundamental units that make up all matter; composed of protons, neutrons, and electrons; an element (see *Focus On Middle School Chemistry Student Textbook*), 29, 30

aurora (ə-rôr'-ə) ● streamers or arches of light that appear in the upper atmosphere when the Earth's magnetic field traps particles that have been charged by a solar storm; also called northern and southern lights, 22

axis (ak'-səs) [plural axes (ak'-sēz)] ● an imaginary straight line around which an object rotates, 17, 23

Barnard's star ● the next nearest star to our solar system after the stars in the Alpha Centauri system, 52

barred spiral galaxy ● see galaxy, barred spiral

basalt (bə-sôlt') ● a dense, fine-grained igneous rock formed from hardened lava from volcanoes, 25-26

belt ● a dark band on a gaseous planet; believed to be made of lower and warmer clouds of gas, 36–37, 38

black hole ● a section in space where, due to extremely high gravity, no light can escape; thought to occur when a large amount of mass from a stellar remnant occupies a small amount of space, 77–78, 81

breccia (bre′-chē-ə) ● a type of rock formed from soil and pieces of rock squeezed together under high heat and pressure, 25–26

calorie (ka′-lə-rē) ● a unit of measurement of energy, 31

Canis Major (kā′-nəs mā′-jər) ● "The Big Dog," a constellation that contains VY CMa, the largest visible star, 53, 54

celestial (sə-les′-chəl) ● having to do with outer space, 2, 7

celestial (sə-les′-chəl) **body** ● an object that exists in space, 2, 7

central bulge ● see galactic bulge

charge, negative ● when an atom has gained an electron and thus has more electrons than protons, it has a negative charge (see *Focus On Middle School Physics Student Textbook*), 29

charge, positive ● when an atom has lost an electron and thus has more protons than electrons, it has a positive charge (see *Focus On Middle School Physics Student Textbook*), 29

charged particles ● particles that carry an electric charge (see *Focus On Middle School Physics Student Textbook*), 21

chemistry (ke′-mə-strē) ● the field of science that studies the composition, structure and properties of matter, 4, 7, 29

Circumstellar Habitable Zone (sər-kəm-ste′-lər ha′-bə-tə-bəl zōn) ● the area of a solar system where an Earth-like planet would be at the right temperature to be suited for life as we know it, 56–57

cold planet ● a planet that is far away from its sun, 56

comet (cä′-mət) ● a celestial body that is a large chunk of dirty ice, 47

compound telescope ● see telescope, compound

constellation (kän-stə-lā′-shən) ● a group of stars that forms a pattern in the sky, 3–4, 53, 54, 57

Copernicus (kō-pər′-ni-kəs), **Nicolaus** ● (1473-1543) the astronomer who reintroduced the idea of a heliocentric cosmos, 7

core ● the inner-most layer of Earth, the Moon, and other celestial bodies; for Earth and the Moon—believed to be made of iron and nickel, 27

cosmos (käz′-mōs) ● our solar system; more broadly, the orderly, harmonious system that includes everything that exists in space—the universe, 4, 5

crater ● a bowl-shaped depression around the opening of a volcano; a hole in the ground from a meteorite impact, 27, 47

crust ● the outer shell of the Earth or the Moon; made of rocks and soil, 27

dwarf planet ● a celestial body that orbits the Sun and has a spherical shape but is too small to disturb the orbits of other planets, 40, 41

Earth ● the planet we live on, 15–23, 33, 34, 40, 41, 43, 44–45, 48, 49

earthquake ● a shaking of the earth caused by the movement of pieces of the crust, 26

eclipse ● see lunar eclipse, solar eclipse

Einstein (ī′-stīn), **Albert** ● (1879-1955) regarded as one of the most influential scientists of all time; the father of modern physics, 31

electric (i-lek'-trik) **charge** ● the gain or loss of electrons resulting in an electric charge (see *Focus On Middle School Physics Student Textbook*), 29

electric (i-lek'-trik) **field** ● a region that is electrically charged, 4

electron (i-lek'-trän) ● one of the three fundamental particles that make up atoms; has almost no mass compared to protons and neutrons, and it carries a negative electric charge; electrons form the bonds between atoms in molecules (see *Focus On Middle School Chemistry Student Textbook*), 29, 30, 77

element (e'-lə-mənt) ● an atom; basic unit of matter (see *Focus On Middle School Chemistry Student Textbook*), 25, 28, 31, 33

elliptical (i-lip'-ti-kəl) ● not fully circular, 44, 49

elliptical galaxy ● see galaxy, elliptical

emission nebula ● see nebula, emission

equator (i-kwā'-tər) ● the imaginary line around the Earth or other planet that divides it into a north half (northern hemisphere) and a south half (southern hemisphere), 16, 17

exoplanet (ek'-sō-pla-nət) ● a planet that orbits a star outside our solar system, 55-56, 57

extrasolar planet ● see exoplanet

first quarter moon ● a phase of the Moon where the Moon looks like a half circle, 19

focal length ● the distance from a lens to its focal point, 11

focal point ● the spot at which rays of light entering a lens come together and produce an image, 10, 11

full moon ● the phase of the Moon during which the Moon looks like a full circle, 19

fusion ● see hydrogen fusion, thermonuclear fusion

galactic (gə-lak'-tic) ● having to do with a galaxy, 61-62, 64, 65

galactic (gə-lak'-tic) **bulge** ● a large, tightly packed group of stars that is the central part of a galaxy (also called the central bulge), 61, 62, 65, 68-72

galactic habitable zone (gə-lak'-tic ha'-bə-tə-bəl zōn) ● the part of a galaxy where conditions might be favorable for life as we know it, 64, 65

galactic (gə-lak'-tic) **halo** ● a spherical group of old stars and gas that surrounds a galaxy, 61-62, 68

galaxy (ga'-lək-sē) ● a large collection of stars, gas, dust, planets, and other objects held together by its own gravity, 60-65, 67-72

galaxy, barred spiral ● similar to a spiral galaxy, but the spiral arms originate at the ends of a bar-shaped region that goes through the center of the galactic bulge, 68, 69-70, 72

galaxy, elliptical (i-lip'-ti-kəl) ● an ellipse shaped congregate of stars with the largest density of stars in the middle of the galaxy; does not have arms or a galactic bulge, 61, 68, 71, 72

galaxy, irregular ● a galaxy that does not fit into one of the other categories, 61, 68, 71-72

Galaxy, Milky Way ● see Milky Way Galaxy

galaxy, spiral ● a galaxy that has a galactic bulge with spiral arms coming out from it making it look similar to a pinwheel, 61-62, 65, 68-69, 70, 72

Galileo ● Galileo Galilei (ga-lə-lā'-ō gal-ə-lā'); (1564-1642) an Italian scientist considered to be the first modern astronomer, 5, 7, 10

gas ● a substance whose molecules are widely separated from each other as in air or water vapor, 28

Gaspra ● see Asteroid Gaspra

geocentric (jē-ō-sen'-trik) ● [*ge,* Gr., earth or land; *kentron,* Gr., point or center] having the Earth as the center, 5, 7

gravitational (gra-və-tā'-shə-nəl) **force** ● the force exerted by objects on one another—the Earth's gravitational force keeps objects on its surface, 19-20, 26

gravity (gra'-və-tē) ● the force exerted by objects on one another (see *Focus On Middle School Physics Student Textbook*), 4, 16, 23, 26, 44, 78

Habitable Zone, Circumstellar ● see Circumstellar Habitable Zone

habitable zone, galactic ● see galactic habitable zone

Hale-Bopp Comet ● a comet that passed close to Earth in 1997, 47-48

Halley's Comet ● a comet that in 1986 passed close enough to Earth for spacecraft to gather information about it, 47-48

heliocentric (hē-lē-ō-sen'-trik) ● [*helios,* Gr., sun; *kentron,* Gr., point or center] having the Sun as the center, 6-7

heliocentric cosmos (hē-lē-ō-sen'-trik käz'-mōs) ● sun-centered solar system; proposed by Aristarchus of Samos and confirmed by Galileo, 6-7

helium (hē'-lē-əm) ● a gas that has two protons, two neutrons, and two electrons (see *Focus On Middle School Chemistry Student Textbook*), 28-31, 75, 79, 81

Herschel (hər'-shəl), **William** ● (1738-1822) a British astronomer who in 1785 presented a paper about the size and shape of our galaxy, 60

hot planet ● a planet that is close to its sun, 56

Hubble classification ● a way of categorizing the various types of galaxies; created by Edwin Hubble, 68-71, 72

Hubble, Edwin ● (1889-1953) an astronomer who discovered that there are galaxies outside the Milky Way and in 1936 devised a method of classifying galaxies, 68

Hubble Space Telescope ● a telescope that is in orbit around the Earth outside the atmosphere, 12, 77

hydrogen (hī'-drə-jən) ● a gas that is the simplest atom, made up of one proton and one electron; a hydrogen atom that has lost its electron can be called a proton (see *Focus On Middle School Chemistry Student Textbook*), 28-31, 75, 76

hydrogen fusion (hī'-drə-jən fyü'-zhən) ● the fusing of hydrogen nuclei under extremely high temperature and pressure, causing a massive amount of energy to be released; also called thermonuclear fusion, 29-31, 75-76

IAU ● see International Astronomical Union

inertia (in-ər'-shə) ● the tendency of things to resist a change in motion (see *Focus On Middle School Physics Student Textbook*), 4

inner solar system ● see solar system, inner

International Astronomical Union (IAU) ● a group of professional astronomers from around the world that determines how celestial bodies should be defined and classified, 4, 40-41

interstellar (in-tər-ste'-lər)● located among the stars, 79

ionize (ī'-ə-nīz) ● to separate the electron(s) from the nucleus of an atom (see *Focus On Middle School Chemistry Student Textbook,* 29

irregular galaxy ● see galaxy, irregular

Jovian planet (jō′-vē-ən pla′-nət) ● a large planet that is similar to Jupiter; also called a gas giant; Jupiter, Saturn, Uranus, and Neptune, 33, 36–39, 41, 43, 44, 45, 49, 56

Jupiter (jü′-pə-tər) ● a large, gaseous planet in the Earth's solar system; also, a massive exoplanet that has Jupiter-like (Jovian) characteristics, 33, 36–37, 40, 41, 43, 44, 45, 48, 49, 56

kpc ● kiloparsec, 1,000 parsecs, 63, 65

kelvin ● a unit of measurement of temperature; 1 kelvin = 273.15 degrees Celcius, 28

Kepler, Johannes ● (1571-1630), German astronomer; developed the laws of planetary motion to describe how the planets move around the Sun, 56

Kepler space telescope ● launched into an orbit around the Sun in March 2009 with the purpose of finding Earth-size and smaller planets orbiting stars in the Milky Way Galaxy, 56

kiloparsec (kpc) ● 1,000 parsecs, 63, 65

Kleopatra ● see Asteroid Kleopatra

Kuiper (kī′-per) **Belt** ● a belt of small celestial bodies orbiting beyond Neptune, 40

Lalande 21185 ● one of the stars that is nearest to our solar system, 52

lander ● a robotic spaceship that can land on the surface of planets or asteroids to capture images and collect data, 12, 13

last quarter moon ● a phase of the Moon where the Moon looks like a half circle, 19

Lippershey, Hans ● a Dutch lens maker who in 1608 filed the first patent for a telescope, 10

luminosity (lü-mə-nä′-sə-tē) ● the amount of electromagnetic energy a celestial body radiates, 63, 75–76

lunar (lü′-nər) ● [*luceo,* L., to shine bright] having to do with the Moon, 3, 25

lunar eclipse (lü′-nər i-klips′) ● a darkening of the Moon as the Moon passes behind the Earth and the Earth's shadow falls on the Moon, 15, 22

Lutetia ● see Asteroid Lutetia

M31 (Messier 31) ● see Andromeda Galaxy

M81 ● see Messier 81

magnetic field ● the area of force surrounding charged particles (see *Focus On Middle School Physics Student Textbook*); for Earth, comes out from the poles and extends into space, interacting with the Sun, 4, 21, 22, 27

magnitude (mag′-nə-tüd) ● a measurement of brightness of a celestial body, 54

mantle ● the layer of a terrestrial planet or moon that is below the crust, 27

mare (mär′-ā), *plural,* maria (mär′-ē-ə) ● [*marinus,* L., sea] one of the dark areas on the Moon that early astronomers thought were bodies of water but are actually lava flows, 27, 31

maria ● see mare

Mariner 4, 6 and 7 ● space probes that photographed Mars, 36

Mariner 10 ● a space probe that has photographed Mercury, 34

Mars ● a terrestrial planet, the fourth from the Sun in our solar system, 33, 34, 35–36, 40, 41, 43, 44, 45, 49

mass ● the property that makes matter resist being moved; commonly, the weight of a substance or object, (see *Focus On Middle School Physics Student Textbook*), 4, 16, 19–20, 26, 30–31

Mercury (mər'-kyə-rē) ● a terrestrial planet; the closest planet to the Sun in our solar system, 33, 34, 41, 43, 44, 45, 49

Messier 31 (M31) ● see Andromeda Galaxy

Messier 81 (M81) ● a spiral galaxy found in the constellation Ursa Major, 69

meteor (mē'-tē-ər) ● a small asteroid that has entered the Earth's atmosphere, 47

meteorite (mē'-tē-ə-rīt) ● a meteor that has reached the Earth's surface, 47

Milky Way Galaxy ● the barred spiral galaxy that contains our solar system, 60-65, 70

mineral ● a naturally formed solid substance that is inorganic (does not contain carbon) and has a highly ordered internal structure of atoms, 25

moon ● [*menas*, Gr., month] a celestial body that orbits a planet, 15, 18-20, 21, 22, 23, 25-27, 31, 48

NGC 224 ● see Andromeda Galaxy

nebula (ne'-byə-lə) (*plural*, nebulae (ne'-byə-lē]) ● [L., cloud] a fuzzy-looking patch of dust, gases, and ionized matter in interstellar space, 79-80, 81

nebula, emission ● a glowing cloud of interstellar matter primarily made up of dust and ionized gases, 80

nebula, planetary ● a nebula that occurs when a supernova collapses and ultraviolet radiation ionizes the surrounding area, 80

negative charge ● see charge, negative

Neptune ● a Jovian planet, eighth from the Sun in the Earth's solar system; also, a less massive exoplanet that has Jupiter-like (Jovian) characteristics, 33, 36, 38, 39, 40, 41, 43, 44, 45, 49, 56

neutron (nü'-trän) ● one of the three fundamental particles that make atoms; it is found in the nucleus and carries no electric charge—it is "neutral" (see *Focus On Middle School Chemistry Student Textbook*), 29, 30, 77

neutron (nü'-trän) **star** ● the remains of a supernova; a stellar remnant, 77, 78

new moon ● the phase of the Moon during which the Moon looks totally dark, 19

Newton, Isaac ● (1643-1727) famous British astronomer and mathematician; the founder of physics, 11

Newtonian telescope ● see telescope, Newtonian

Norma Arm ● one of the minor spiral arms of the Milky Way Galaxy, 62

North Pole ● the northern end of the Earth's axis; the most northern point on Earth, 16, 17

North Star ● the star that appears to be directly over the North Pole of the Earth; also called Polaris, 2

northern hemisphere (he'-mə-sfir) ● the northern half of the Earth, 3

northern lights ● auroras in the northern hemisphere, 22

nova (nō'-və) (*plural*, novae [nō'-vē]) ● [L., new] a white dwarf star that increases and decreases in brightness as it takes hydrogen from neighboring stars and uses it for thermonuclear fusion, 75-76, 81

nuclear (nü'-klē-ər) **reaction** ● occurs when the protons and neutrons of an atom are moved in and out of the nucleus, creating energy and changing the structure of the atom, 4, 30

nucleus (nü'-klē-əs) *plural*, nuclei (nü'-klē-ī) ● the central portion of an atom that houses the protons and neutrons, 29

obliquity ● see orbital obliquity

Opportunity ● a rover that landed on Mars in 2004, 13

orbit ● the curved path of a celestial body as it travels around another celestial body, 5, 44, 45, 49

orbital obliquity (or'-bə-təl ō-bli'-kwə-tē) ● the tilt of the Earth's axis, 17, 20, 23

Orion (ə-rī'-ən) ● a constellation that looks like a hunter with a belt, club, and shield, 3, 53

Orion (ə-rī'-ən) **Arm** ● the small, partial spiral arm where Earth resides in the Milky Way Galaxy, 62, 65

outer solar system ● see solar system, outer

parsec (pär'-sec) ● a unit of measure used by astronomers; equals 206,260 AUs, 52, 57

Perseus (pər'-sŭs, pər'-sē-əs) **Arm** ● one of the major spiral arms of the Milky Way Galaxy, 62, 65

phases of the moon ● the changes in the Moon's appearance as it is viewed from Earth, 2, 19

physics (fi'-ziks) ● [*physika*, Gr., physical or natural] the field of science that investigates the basic laws of the natural world, 4, 7, 29

planet ● [*planetai*, Gr., wanderer] a large spherical celestial body that orbits a sun, has enough mass to have its own gravity, and has cleared its orbit of other celestial bodies, 16, 23

planet, cold ● a planet that is far from its sun, 56

planet, hot ● a planet that is close to its sun, 56

planetary nebula ● see nebula, planetary

plate ● a very large piece of the Earth's crust; its movement can cause earthquakes, 27

Pluto (plü'-tō) ● once considered the 9th planet, is now classified as a dwarf planet or plutoid; this re-classification is in dispute, 33, 39–41

plutoid (plü'-toid) ● a celestial body that has enough gravity to have formed a spherical shape, has not cleared its orbit, and exists beyond the orbit of Neptune, 41

positive charge ● see charge, positive

probe ● see space probe

proton (prō'-tän) ● one of the three fundamental particles that make atoms; carries a positive electric charge (see *Focus On Middle School Chemistry Student Textbook*), 29–30, 77

proton, hydrogen ● see hydrogen

Proxima Centauri (präk'-sə-mə sen-tô'-rē) ● the star that is nearest to our solar system; part of the Alpha Centauri system, 52, 57

pulsating star ● a star whose luminosity (brightness) changes with time; a variable star, 63

red giant star ● a star that has used up its hydrogen during thermonuclear fusion and becomes hotter, bigger and brighter as it burns helium, 75, 81

red hypergiant star ● a massive red star that has a diameter of between 100 and 2100 times that of our Sun and that may be thousands to millions times brighter than the Sun, 54

reflector telescope ● see telescope, reflector

refractor telescope ● see telescope, refractor

rover ● a robotic spaceship that can land on the surface of a planet or asteroid and then travel around, capturing images and collecting data, 12, 13

Sagittarius (sa-jə-ter'-ē-əs) **Arm** ● one of the minor spiral arms of the Milky Way Galaxy, 62, 65

telescope, compound ● a telescope that combines elements of refractor and reflector telescopes, 10, 11

telescope, Newtonian ● a common reflector telescope named after Isaac Newton, 11

telescope, reflector ● a telescope that uses a combination of mirrors and lenses to focus incoming light and magnify an image, 10, 11

telescope, refractor ● a telescope with a lens at one end and an eyepiece at the other; light entering through the lens is bent, magnifying the image, 10, 11

terra (ter'-ə); *plural*, terrae (ter'-ē) ● [*terra*, L., land] a light area on the Moon's surface that contains rugged craters, 27, 31

terrestrial (tə-res'-trē-əl) ● (*terra*, L., earth) Earth-like; relating to the Earth, 33, 44

terrestrial planet (tə-res'-trē-əl pla'-nət) ● a planet that is Earth-like; made of rocky materials and closer to our Sun; Mercury, Venus, Earth and Mars, 33–36, 41, 43, 44, 45, 49

thermonuclear fusion (thər-mō-nü'-clē-ər fyü'-zhən) ● the fusing of hydrogen nuclei under extremely high temperature and pressure, causing a massive amount of energy to be released; process used by our Sun to create energy; also called hydrogen fusion, 29–31, 75–76

thick disk ● in a galaxy, an area that contains older stars and surrounds the thin disk, 61, 62

thin disk ● in a galaxy, an area that contains the majority of stars in the galaxy and orbits the galactic bulge, 61–62, 65

tide ● the rise and fall of ocean levels due to gravitational forces of the Moon and the Sun, 20, 21, 23

Tombaugh, Clyde ● an astronomer who discovered Pluto in 1930, 39–40

universe ● our solar system; more broadly, everything that exists in space; the cosmos, 4, 6, 7

Uranus (yür'-ə-nəs) ● a Jovian planet, seventh from the Sun in the Earth's solar system; contains a significant amount of methane, giving it a bluish color; 33, 36, 38–39, 40, 41, 43, 44, 45, 49

VY Canis Majoris (VY CMa) ● a red hypergiant star that is the largest star visible in the night sky, 54–55

vacuum (va' kyüm) ● in astronomy, containing no matter, 26

vaporize (vā'-pə-rīz) ● to turn a substance into its gaseous state, 47

variable star ● a star whose luminosity (brightness) changes with time; a pulsating star, 63

Venus (vē'-nəs) ● a terrestrial planet, the second from the Sun in the Earth's solar system, 33, 34, 35, 40, 41, 43, 44, 45, 49

Viking 1 ● a lander that captured the first image of the surface of Mars, 13

Voyager 1 ● a space probe launched in 1977; is now outside our solar system, 12–13

Voyager 2 ● a space probe that photographed Neptune in 1989, 39

waning crescent moon ● a phase of the Moon where it looks crescent shaped, 19

waning gibbous (ji'-bəs *or* gi'-bəs) moon ● a phase of the Moon where the Moon looks convex in shape, 19

waxing crescent moon ● a phase of the Moon where it looks crescent shaped, 19

waxing gibbous (jiʹ-bəs *or* giʹ-bəs) **moon** ● a phase of the Moon where the Moon looks convex in shape, 19

white dwarf star ● a star that has used up all of its fuel, leaving just its core, 75, 76, 81

Wolf 359 ● one of the stars that is nearest to our solar system, 52

zone ● a light band on a gaseous planet believed to be made of lower and warmer clouds of gas, 36-37, 38, 39

Pronunciation Key

a	add	ī	ice	r	run
ā	race	j	joy	s	sea
ä	palm	k	cool	sh	sure
â(r)	air	l	love	t	take
b	bat	m	move	u	up
ch	check	n	nice	ü	sue
d	dog	ng	sing	v	vase
e	end	o	odd	w	way
ē	tree	ō	open	y	yarn
f	fit	ô	jaw	z	zebra
g	go	oi	oil	ə	a in above
h	hope	oo	pool		e in sicken
i	it	p	pit		i in possible
					o in melon
					u in circus